The Personal Power Roadmap

THE ULTIMATE 7 STEP SYSTEM TO EFFECTIVELY
SOLVE PROBLEMS, MAKE DECISIONS, AND REACH
YOUR GOALS

Marjory Harris

Marjory Harris / The Personal Power Roadmap
Personalpowerroadmap.com

Cover Design and Multi Tool Graphic by Bob Matthews, Matthews Design Group

Book Layout ©2013 BookDesignTemplates.com

The Personal Power Roadmap/Marjory Harris
ISBN-13:
978-1530548460

ISBN-10:
1530548462

Disclaimer: The information in this book is based on my own experience. It is not intended as a substitute for the advice of trained medical or mental health professionals. The reader should regularly consult a physician, therapist or counselor in matters relating to his/her physical or mental health and particularly regarding any symptoms that may require diagnosis or medical attention. If you use any of the information in this book, the author and the publisher assume no responsibility for your actions.

Thank you for reading my book.

BONUS: Here are the links for your downloadable customizable forms and mind maps and the instructions on how to use The Personal Power Roadmap with Evernote:

For the Roadmap chart in 4 formats:
www.personalpowerroadmap.com/templates

To download the mind maps and see screenshots of the ones from this book: www.personalpowerroadmap.com/mind-maps

Instructions on how to use The Personal Power Roadmap with Evernote:
www.personalpowerroadmap.com/evernote-ppr

A SPECIAL GIFT: Download the "START NOW" questions in a 2-page chart: www.personalpowerroadmap.com/start-now

To my mentors who taught me how to make decisions, solve problems, and set goals:

Dr. Leslie John Adkins, who taught me that change may be "difficult but not impossible," Harland Hand, who taught me that problems are an opportunity to be creative and have fun, and Michael Hyatt, who inspired me to publish this book.

Contents

The Personal Power Roadmap is a system for problem solving, decision making, goal setting, and project development. It relies on three essential skills we are born with – imagination, cognition, and motivation, techniques for honing these essential skills, and exercises to show you how to use them. A unique, customizable chart ("Roadmap") comes in four formats and can be used on multiple platforms, devices, or on paper.

In Chapter 1, "Life's Flat Tires: Everyone Has Them," you will discover the basic concept and some principles for success with the Personal Power Roadmap system. You will learn about the 3 Essential Skills and how the Personal Power Roadmap relies on the synergy the skills create when used together. You will learn a technique for increasing your motivation by using the other two Essential Skills. Six exercises let you put in motion these skills and build your confidence.

In Chapter 2, "Take the First Steps to Successful Problem Solving," you will learn to define problems so you can solve them. You will also learn how to make decisions, set goals, and outline projects. You will discover and start using "START NOW," the eight questions that get you on the road to success.

In Chapter 3, "The Power of the Roadmap Chart," you will learn how to use the Personal Power Roadmap for different purposes, what formats are available and how to store your Roadmaps. You will see examples of Personal Powemr Roadmaps to plan and track effective decision making, problem solving, goal setting, and project creation.

In Chapter 4, "Imagine That! Imagination is the First Essential Skill," you will learn four techniques with variations for honing your imaginative skill. You will imagine yourself in a future time and place so you can use that image to design your Roadmap. You will practice how to know it, see it and believe it, to find out what you *really* want.

In Chapter 5, "Figure it Out! Cognition is the Second Essential Skill," you will learn how to use cognition to work with imagination. You'll use the two together to craft workable solutions and Personal Power Roadmaps for making decisions, solving problems, setting goals, and creating change. You will learn powerful techniques for supercharging learning, research and storage.

In Chapter 6, "Move Along the Path to Success: Motivation is the Third Essential Skill," you will learn how to use techniques to supercharge your engine so you are energized to get going. You will learn a technique that uses all 3 Essential Skills for creating an instantaneous good habit to achieve success.

In Chapter 7, "Get Unstuck and Get Going Again," you will learn how to get going again if you are stuck. You will learn the elements of cognitive therapy – how to overcome negative thoughts, the enemies of effective problem solving and change. You will learn how to remove "malware of the mind," how to end procrastination, and how to get out of the perfectionism trap.

In Chapter 8, "Applying the Personal Power Roadmap to Life's Flat Tires," I show you case histories and specific applications of the Personal Power Roadmap concept. You will see the skills in action, how they interact and interrelate when working with the Personal Power Roadmap.

In Chapter 9, "The Challenge of Change," you meet two remarkable men who were my mentors in problem solving.

Each chapter includes a summary of the Key Points and What You Will Learn in the Next Chapter. You can find the exercises, techniques, case histories, and a summary of key points in the Index.

Part One

Introduction, Life's Flat Tires, Take the First Steps & The Power of the Roadmap Chart

Introduction

Do you need help solving life's problems? We all do!

Most of us grew up without learning any system for dealing with the common problems we all face – life's flat tires. Most of us learn the hard way, in the School of Hard Knocks.

There is an easier way. The Personal Power Roadmap is a practical, proven multi tool for making decisions, solving problems, setting goals, and creating projects. This book shows how to tap into and use the 3 Essential Skills you already have – imagination, cognition, and motivation – to get you where you want to go.

In this book, you'll learn:

- A 7-step system to use on every problem or goal to get clarity on exactly what you need to do.
- How to tap into your 3 inner problem-solving skills with simple exercises and techniques.
- A method that is action oriented, not theoretical.
- How to be proactive, not just reactive.
- The powerful START NOW questions that get you the clarity you need to be successful.
- 10 common mental deceptions that keep you stuck and Cognitive Behavioral Therapy techniques to remove this "malware of the mind."
- Practical methods for finally overcoming the procrastination and perfectionism keeping you from a better life.

- The psychology of how to swap out a bad habit for a good one.
- A method for making major life changes without getting completely overwhelmed.
- Real world case studies to show you exactly how this flexible system can be used to solve a business problem, find a mate, declutter and organize a room, lose weight, and more.

You only need to learn one method, one time. I will show you how with easy-to-do exercises, techniques and case histories you can apply to any of life's challenges.

Change is challenging and may seem impossible when you start your journey, but as my mentor, Dr. Adkins, said, "It is difficult but not impossible." Read more about him in Chapter 9, "The Challenge of Change." I got through many a rough patch remembering his words.

As Dr. Bruce Leckart, Ph.D., observed: "This book is easy to read, easy to follow and provides a way of getting your head in a place where you can really improve your life. It's like having your own therapist without all the complications."

Solomon "Sandy" Perlo, M.D., who specializes in Psychiatry and Chronic Pain Medicine, wrote: "The Personal Power Roadmap is a concise and practical 'how to do it' guide I highly recommend to my patients and others. This book with its tools and chart is an easy to learn method that works for many kinds of problems, for the individual or couples or even groups."

Marta Vukasovic, executive with a Fortune 100 company, recommends The Personal Power Roadmap as "an essential tool in every process leader's tool chest. This tool unlocks the problem-solving potential in every individual, removes the procrastination, fear and anxiety often associated with dealing with problems. It enables you to resume control. The most exciting thing about this tool is that everyone who embarks on this journey, regardless of their age, profession, or background, will achieve excellence in effective problem solving."

Rebecca Kitchings, Entrepreneur and Small Business Owner, wrote: "By the end of this book with its honest and humorous life stories, you will have a new confidence in your ability to manage the various obstacles in your professional and personal life. The tools will help you *create* that fork in the road you should be on."

Try it and see. Road test it on a current "flat tire" in your life and experience how easy it is to use the Personal Power Roadmap to change your life and get going on life's highway.

Author Marjory Harris has been a social worker, lawyer, counselor, and founder of Multidimensional Problem Solving^sm. She has master's degrees in psychology and literature and a juris doctor degree in law. For 50 years she has helped others discover their innate abilities and a fresh perspective on life.

How to Use This Book

This book has three parts:

In Part One you will learn the basics and how to use the Personal Power Roadmap.

In Part Two you will learn techniques for honing the 3 Essential Skills so you can use them to create synergy.

In Part Three you will learn how to get unstuck, how to apply the Personal Power Roadmap method to real-life problems, and what I learned from two remarkable mentors.

Each chapter builds on the previous one, giving you a fuller understanding of what works and why. I recommend you work through the book chapter by chapter. Even if you skip around and just read parts of the book, you will benefit.

You will find additional materials online:
See www.personalpowerroadmap.com/templates for the Roadmap chart in 4 formats. Instructions on how to use the chart in Evernote are here: www.personalpowerroadmap.com/evernote-ppr. To use mind maps and see screenshots of the ones from this book, go to: www.personalpowerroadmap.com/mind-maps.

A Multi Tool Icon Highlights the Content

Stories & Case Histories: Spare Tire

Exercises: Jack

Techniques: Lug Wrench

Explanations & Theories: Flashlight

Key Points & Action Steps: Key

1

Life's Flat Tires: Everyone Has Them

How many people does it take to change a flat tire?

On a cold snowy night in the dead of winter, a car got a flat tire on a little traveled road in a small town. In the car were three "brains" from the local high school. None knew how to change a flat tire. Fortunately a car came along with a local "jock" who knew how to change a flat tire. The three brains were soon on their way to their warm homes.

I was one of the smart kids in the car who had no idea how to change a flat tire. We felt pretty stupid. We knew what was wrong but not how to fix it.

It didn't help that the tools were in the trunk of the car with the spare tire. We had no directions so the tools alone were not enough. This was long before cell phones and Triple A. I huddled in the car as my two friends paced in the snow and debated what to do. We were so relieved when the jock showed up.

We all have the tools for problem solving, but not the directions. The tools are three essential skills we are born with. The directions are in this book.

The fact is, problem solving has little to do with being smart or having a high IQ. It is about having a method that works. It is about having practical knowledge. And this is something anyone can learn.

So the answer to the question above is, it takes only one person to change a flat tire, if he or she has the necessary tools and knows how to do it.

Everyone has problems, and they fall into general categories:

1. Work & Careers
2. Money & Finance
3. Love & Relationships
4. Health & Body Image
5. Productivity & Goals
6. Unhappiness & Dissatisfaction
7. Bad Habits & Failure to Create Good Ones

I call these common problems "flat tires." With a real flat tire, if you don't know how to fix it or didn't bring the right tools with you, you call for help. Think of the Personal Power Roadmap as readily accessible roadside assistance for life's flat tires.

Flat Tires That Happen In Life

Here are a few examples of flat tires on our journey:

Work & Career:

You didn't get the job you wanted, or the job you got isn't going well. You didn't get the promotion you deserved, or you got no raise. What was once your dream job is now a nightmare. Or you lost interest altogether in your chosen career.

Money & Finance:

You want to increase your income but don't know how. Or maybe you make good money but have no savings or disastrous investments.

Love & Relationships:

You want a meaningful relationship but don't know how to find or create one. Or you're in a relationship but want more commitment. Or you want to end the relationship because you believe it will never work.

Health & Body Image:

You know you need to lose weight, but now the doctor says you have prediabetes, so you can't put off doing something. You broke your leg and ruined your chances to be in a marathon. You are getting older, but you're having a hard time accepting it.

Productivity & Goals:

You want to get more done, you want to create positive change so you can lead a better life, but life gets in the way. Time ticks on and you stay the same.

Unhappiness & Dissatisfaction:

You feel you're a failure, or not as successful as you should be. You feel that something is missing, or you got what you wanted but it isn't enough. You want to transform but don't know how.

Bad Habits & Failure to Create Good Ones:

You try to stop smoking, lose weight, or start exercising. How many years of New Year's resolutions ticked by while you struggled to figure out how? Or you knew how, but didn't do it or do it enough to make a difference.

What Successful People Know That You Can Learn

Did you ever wonder why some people seem to take the easy path through life while you learn everything the hard way, in the School of Hard Knocks?

Did they go to better schools? Have a higher IQ? Have better luck?

Try "none of the above." While it may help to have a better education and parents that expect you to achieve, it may have the opposite effect and turn you into an underachiever. And luck benefits those who seize the opportunities it presents. When you have a spare moment, Google "pet rock." A chance idea – a ridiculous one – turned Gary Dahl into a million-aire, because *he acted on the idea.*

Successful people all know a secret. They endorse what Carl Jung said: "I am not what happened to me, I am what I choose to become." They consciously elect a path to take, then go into action. With the Personal Power Roadmap, you can learn to do this too.

> Successful people know that when you do nothing, nothing good can happen, and you stay stuck. But when you commit to change and consistently take effective action, you get to where you want to go. You gain personal power.

While everyone has flat tires in their lives, successful people don't wait for problems to arise. They plan what they want to achieve, and so can you. When successful people are caught up in a problem, they quickly switch gears, go into action, and fix their problems. You can do this too. You can react more effectively. You can be proactive and use the system in this book to create positive change.

The Personal Power Roadmap

The Personal Power Roadmap is a flexible multi tool that works on many types of problems, decisions, goals or projects. You can use the Personal Power Roadmap alone, with an accountability buddy, with someone else working on the same problem, or with a team of people.

The Personal Power Roadmap allows you to think more creatively and avoid snap decisions, quick fixes, and other problems that flow from not having a systematic approach. You stay focused and on track using special tools: exercises, techniques, questions ("START NOW"), and the unique Roadmap chart.

The Personal Power Roadmap chart comes in four formats and works on multiple platforms. You can download and customize it. You can even work on paper if you like to feel that in your hands rather than an electronic device.

The Personal Power Roadmap is a practical, proactive method that relies on the power of potentiation, the synergistic interaction between two or more of the 3 Essential Skills, resulting in a response greater than the individual responses. Using the skills synergistically increases the power of each individual skill.

The 3 Essential Skills in a Nutshell

The 3 Essential Skills work together to create a powerful problem-solving synergy. They can be practiced or combined in any order.

First Skill: Imagination creates visions

When I was five years old, I watched my mother put out a plate of cookies and a glass of milk on the little table near the fireplace. Stockings were hanging from the mantle and one of them had my name on it. My mother told my sister and me to go to bed, that when we woke up, we'd find the gifts Santa Claus carried down the chimney.

I was so excited I couldn't sleep. I sat at my bedroom window and gazed at the sky. Imagine my joy when I saw Santa Claus driving across the sky in his sled, piled high with gifts, right toward our house.

Reassured he was coming to our rooftop and chimney, I fell asleep. In the morning, I found the gifts under the tree. An empty glass was on the table and the cookie plate was bare, more proof of Santa's coming and going.

We create our reality first in our minds. In Chapter 4 you will learn easy ways to use imagination to know it, see it and believe it.

Second Skill: Cognition creates solutions

When I was in elementary school, I learned how to jump rope. I wasn't any good at it and when they were forming teams, I was the last one to be chosen. Often the bell rang before it was even my turn.

I had plenty of time to watch the other girls jump. I observed whoever brought the rope got to jump over it first. So I went home and took my mother's clothesline out of the backyard and brought it to school. Now I got to jump instead of stand on the sidelines.

We learn by observation, experience, instruction, and research. We develop our essential skill of cognition in various ways. In Chapter 5 you will learn powerful techniques for supercharging learning.

Third Skill: Motivation gets us going

In 1982, I lost my job when my company was acquired by a bigger one. I had casually been looking around before this happened, but with no sense of urgency. As soon as I got the news, I flew into action. Within days I had a workable plan. What motivated me most was fear I would lose my house and garden.

Motivation keeps us wanting to stay alive. In Chapter 6, you will learn how to use techniques to get you energized. The more motivated you are, the sooner changes happen and the better the chances for success.

By practicing the 3 Essential Skills with the techniques and exercises in this book, you can avoid the School of Hard Knocks and go straight to creating a personal Roadmap that will have you traveling with a new, productive itinerary.

What's new gets easier with practice

The Personal Power Roadmap works best when you do it as part of your daily life rather than waiting and turning to it when a crisis occurs. If you incorporate these techniques into your daily routines, they will always work for you and prevent most of life's problems from becoming big ones. If a big problem comes out of the blue, the tools will come to mind because you created a habit.

Technique for Chapter 1

Increase Your Motivation Using 2 Other Essential Skills

The less you're motivated, the more you need to hone the motivation skill. Try this easy technique to increase motivation:

> **Use your imagination and cognition skills and write about your favorite meal. As you jot down the items, think how much you enjoy the food. Are you hungry? Do you want to raid the fridge or call for takeout? Congratulations! You instantly increased your motivation by using imagination and cognition.**

Why does this work? As you imagine something and think about it, you are priming the pump, activating desire to accomplish something – in this case to eat. You can use this technique for something you need to do but want to avoid. In Chapter 6 you will learn techniques to supercharge your engine so you are energized to get going.

Exercises for Chapter 1

For the best results, find a quiet place, get into a comfortable position, and close your eyes before jump-starting your imagination.

Begin Your Journey with Baby Steps

You were born with the ability to walk, but you didn't come running out of the womb. It takes the average baby 4 to 6 months to roll over, 7 to 9 months to sit up, and it's usually around 11 months before the baby tries to walk on its own.

The baby starts with crawling. It then pulls itself up until it can stand upright, then steps forward, falls and tries again. With parents encouraging each stage, the baby keeps trying despite the falls and soon gains confidence and strength.

This process is repeated until one day, without support, the baby takes its first real steps across the room and falls into the loving arms of its parents.

Exercise 1-1: Learning to Walk

Imagine this: You are this baby, about to take those first steps. You are determined to walk upright. You will do it even if you fall with every other step. You are creating your world with joy and expectation. You do not know limits, you are not filled with doubt.

You take those first steps to develop your legs and your sense of balance, so you can move forward. You don't give up trying to walk just because you fall every few steps. Something in you knows that with persistence, you will walk without difficulty.

Now imagine yourself as the proud parent, reaching out to the baby, knowing that falls are part of the process, delighted with your baby's progress. You are filled with joy that your baby is walking, you are reaching out with open arms, encouraging this child who is eager to come to you. Like the child, there is a look of joy on your face. This child is your hope for the future.

We are all both baby and parent. By exercising your imagination and focusing on the positive potential of your own first steps, you will see you have the ability to learn and to find your own momentum.

Ask yourself these questions:

1. How do you feel about yourself after doing this exercise?
2. Are you pleased that you have brought this delightful child into the world?
3. Do you feel good knowing your baby is making progress in the normal way?
4. Are you beset by fears that your baby will fall and be injured, or do you have other negative thoughts?
5. Do you still have the unbridled optimism of the baby? Or did your life experiences transform that optimism into doubt, fear, and sadness?

If you saw yourself as the baby and then as its parents, you have already used your imagination, one of the 3 Essential Skills you will practice and hone throughout this book. If you didn't do this, please go back now and try it.

Note how it makes you feel as you become the baby, eager to walk forward. You also learned that you get somewhere by taking small steps, one after the other. You learned you need the determination that comes from wanting to succeed.

Avoid the School of Hard Knocks

Why learn by trial and error what you could learn faster with a planned approach? Learn what works by applying techniques that enhance and hone your 3 Essential Skills. You can then work on problems proactively with a practical and systematic method.

Let's illustrate this with an exercise you can use whenever you want to feel relaxed and upbeat.

Exercise 1-2: Planning a Vacation

Imagine this: Your boss tells you that if you don't use your vacation time by the end of next month, you will lose it. He wants a fast response. You rack your brain trying to figure out where to go, Googling without enthusiasm. You grab at something, order a ticket and reserve a room. You feel forced into a joyless vacation by your employer's "use it or lose it" rule.

You planned your vacation using the School of Hard Knocks method. Now let's redo it using the Personal Power Roadmap:

Daydream you are on a tropical beach, listening to the waves hitting the shore and the rustling sound of the palm fronds in the breeze. You hear roosters crowing nearby. You smell the sweet scent of plumeria in bloom. You sip your Mai Tai.

Coming out of your daydream, you Google "palm trees and roosters." Bingo! You are going to Kauai. You add this to your to-do list and calendar "Book travel plans to Kauai."

You see how easily you can do the Personal Power Roadmap techniques? You applied the 3 Essential Skills to a problem. By the time you finish this book, you will have mastered these skills.

Overcome Negativity, the Thief of Motivation

Do you worry about the future, ruminate on the past, and tell yourself sad stories? Do you create a history and project it into the future? Are you trapped in the story you created, one of failure and futility? The same skill of imagination can rescue you from negativity and motivate you to create a new story, one which is positive and energizing.

Exercise 1-3: Food Aisle Temptation

Imagine this: You are at your local grocery store to pick up laundry detergent. You spot a colorful display of a new potato chip. Now you are hungry. There is a moment of happy anticipation as you imagine chewing on these chips. Then you remember you are trying to lose weight, and this will wreck your diet. Your mood sours.

With this exercise, you experienced the ability to change your mind, your feelings, and your mood. And you did this with no effort. Why? Because you were born with this ability.

You can transmute negative thoughts into positive ones, and your mood will change. In Chapter 7, "Get Unstuck and Get Going Again," you learn how to harness this power. For now, when you experience negative thoughts keeping you from your goals or projects, visualize a thief stealing your valuable belongings, your motivation to succeed. Chase the thief away by imagining yourself succeeding at your goal.

Problems Have Built-in Possibilities

If you want to transform problems into changes, you need to take effective action. Nothing changes without change, or as it's often put, "you can't make an omelet without breaking eggs." Put another way, to change something means to make changes. If you see the changes as solutions, you don't focus on the loss.

Exercise 1-4: Breaking Eggs

Imagine your problem is an egg. Think of the possibilities built into it: Will you make something fancy, like a soufflé? Or meringues? Crepes or a Spanish tortilla? Or just a hard or soft-boiled egg? If you are feeling lazy, break a raw egg into a glass, add Worcestershire sauce, hot sauce, vinegar, salt, and pepper, and you have a prairie oyster.

The unbroken egg is just an egg, and it can be served hard or soft-boiled. But the broken egg has endless possibilities. It can be made into omelets, crepes, tortillas, sauces, soups, and drinks.

If you are trapped in a dead end job, you could focus on trying to make the job more likable, but it's still a dead end job (soft or hard boiled eggs). If you focus on making a big career change, you enjoy many more opportunities (omelets, crepes, etc.)

So what are your eggs? What do you want to make with them? Will you be content with small changes, ones you can do with ease, or do you want bigger results?

Solutions are Positive Changes

Problems need change, and problems lead to change. You can make small changes, such as losing 10 pounds when you need to lose 50. Or getting a small raise and staying at the dead end job instead of doing the work required for a more rewarding career. It is up to you.

It takes more effort to change than to stay the same. You need to desire change. It's essential to motivation, one of the 3 Essential Skills. Nothing changes if you don't make changes.

Exercise 1-5: Happiness

Imagine this: Describe your life if you were happy. Would you be rich? Living in a fabulous house? Surfing the blue Pacific, or skiing the slopes of a high-end resort? Write it with enough detail so you can see yourself there, lazing on the beach with a Mai Tai. Capture the smells, sounds, and tactile sensations with your vision. Write at least a page. Then answer these questions:

1. **What steps do you need to take to bring about what you imagined?**

2. **What would you need to change? Include your attitude. Be specific ("I need to see myself as a success instead of a failure").**

3. **Are you willing to put time and effort into reaching your vision of happiness?**

4. **What changes in your present life would make the most difference to achieving your vision?**

Whatever your answer is to number 4, focus your time and energy on this.

Kindling Passion

It's much easier to make changes when you have a passion. It's a fire already burning, not a pile of sticks waiting for a match. But no matter where you are on the continuum between apathy and passion, you can make headway by using two essential skills, imagination and cognition, to increase your level of motivation.

If nothing gets you excited or inspires you to go into action, you need to rid yourself of negative thoughts keeping you back. You need a reason, a "why" that engages you. Can you think of one now? Or do you switch to a negative thought?

Exercise 1-6: On the Train

Imagine a train heading toward the station where you want to go. The train jerks as it travels through a switch. It comes to a stop on a siding. You see other trains on parallel tracks heading to the station. You are stuck on your train, not going anywhere.

Ask yourself, why did your train go through that switch to the siding? What negative thought delayed your journey? Are you worried about what awaits you at the station? Afraid you don't look right? Afraid of the unknown?

Seeing yourself in a negative way and telling yourself sad stories stops you in your tracks. The more you repeat these negative histories to yourself, the more you believe change is hopeless and unattainable, the more failure awaits you.

This book will teach you how to create a new story of a competent, mature and successful person. The more effort you put into your new story, the more success you'll achieve. In the next chapter you'll learn the first steps you need to take for success.

Remember, nothing changes if you don't make changes.

Key Points in This Chapter

The Personal Power Roadmap is a flexible multi tool that works on many types of problems, decisions, goals or projects. It is a practical, proactive method that relies on the power of potentiation, the synergistic interaction between two or more of the 3 Essential Skills. We are born with these Essential Skills – imagination, cognition, and motivation. You have them but need to hone them.

By practicing the 3 Essential Skills with the techniques and exercises in this book, you can avoid the School of Hard Knocks and go straight to creating a personal Roadmap that will have you traveling with a new, productive itinerary.

What You Will Learn In the Next Chapter

In the next chapter, "Take the First Steps to Successful Problem Solving," you will learn how to create a Roadmap that makes change doable. You start with defining a decision or problem so it can be solved and setting goals so they can be achieved. You will learn an essential set of questions – START NOW – that gets you on your way to successful outcomes.

2

Take the First Steps to Successful Problem Solving

Have you ever wondered why some people know how to make big changes quickly while others – maybe you – are agonizing? They seem to have a recipe for success, with some "secret sauce" that works like a charm.

What they have is a method and useful habits, which you can learn too.

"Problem solving" includes making decisions, setting goals, setting up projects, and creating change. Whether it's deciding on a career change, wanting to increase your income, lose weight, remodel the kitchen, or clean out the garage, anything that takes more than a few easy steps or a few hours comes under the label of "problem solving" in this book. All of these require using the 3 Essential Skills, the START NOW questions, the Personal Power Roadmap chart ("Roadmap"), and the exercises and techniques in this book, if you want a fool-proof method for successful problem solving.

Take Baby Steps or Run, but Start With a Soluable Problem

When you pack for a trip, you need to know where you're going. Do you need snorkel gear when trekking in the Himalayas? An umbrella in the Atacama Desert? Before you try problem solving, you need to have a problem you can solve.

Remember Alexander the Great and the Gordian Knot? The Gordian Knot stood in his path. Legend had it that whoever unraveled the intricate knot could conquer Asia, but conquering the knot was impossible. Alexander used the 3 Essential Skills: He imagined himself invincible, letting no obstacle hinder him. He figured out how to eliminate the knot. He cut it apart with his sword. His desire to conquer Asia motivated him to take an unconventional action.

There are different versions of how Alexander got rid of the Gordian knot. Realizing he couldn't unravel the knot, he used his sword to destroy it. In another version, he removed the pole that held the knot in place. He figured out a novel solution by redefining the problem so it could be solved by an action. "Gordian knot" became a proverbial term for a complicated problem solvable only by bold action. Do you have (or imagine) a Gordian Knot problem? What action could you take to conquer the problem? Maybe you need to redefine it, as Alexander did.

The Importance of Focus: What You Need to Do Next

Before you can take effective action in problem solving and creating change, you need to focus. In a panic, our fearful mind wanders everywhere. We cannot access our intuitive or logical mind. By breaking the problem-solving process into separate tasks, we can reign in anxiety. We can think clearly.

My dear friend and mentor, Harland Hand, fought in the Battle of the Bulge in World War II. In the dead of winter, the Germans surprised and overwhelmed the Allied forces. Hand found himself alone in a deserted village trudging through lanes narrowed by snowbanks, cut off from other troops. As he passed dead bodies, he worried about German snipers. An American soldier huddled beside a house trembling and useless, overcome with anxiety, reminded Hand he needed to stay calm in chaos or he too might succumb.

He thought of Aunt Mary, who'd have a cup of coffee and something to eat, tie her apron and take charge. She did what needed to be done without being distracted by anxious thoughts. He learned from her how to focus on the immediate problem, which was what to do next.

Focus on today. As the Dalai Lama said, "There are only two days in the year that nothing can be done. One is called yesterday and the other is called tomorrow, so today is the right day to love, believe, do and mostly live."

When confronting a major problem or life change, it's easy to get overwhelmed by the size of the task ahead. The mind is wandering everywhere, exploring doubts from the past, worries about the future. You need to focus on the present. The only time is now.

The Most Important Step for Success: Create a Personal Power Roadmap

The Personal Power Roadmap is fundamental to your success. Shortcuts won't get you there. The Personal Power Roadmap will.

Think of the Personal Power Roadmap as a valuable, go-to multi tool. You can use it for these purposes, and maybe a few you think up on your own:

- Making a decision
- Solving a problem
- Reaching a goal
- Creating a project

The fact is, all the above have the same things in common:

- You need to define what it is and phrase it in a way so you can accomplish it
- You need to know what your reasons are for doing it

- You need to envision what you want to achieve so you are motivated
- You need to research and analyze
- You need to decide what your next actions are to accomplish the results you desire
- You need to stay on track and not get stuck

Technique for Chapter 2

7 Steps to Working with the Personal Power Roadmap

1. The problem/decision/goal/project ("problem") phrased as solvable
2. The reasons that motivate or impede you
3. How you imagine the future
4. Research and analysis
5. Plan B (fall back or backup plan)
6. Doable, bite-sized actions, with deadlines
7. Progress log of activities and notes

Step 1: Phrase the Problem So It Fits the START NOW Model

The way you phrase the problem creates the solution or invites failure. Let's return to the imaginary problem where you are losing your job. Which of these works best as a "problem phrased as solvable"?

a. Find a new job
b. Update my resume
c. Consider becoming a consultant
d. Explore career opportunities and decide by [insert date in near future] whether to find another job like the current one or set up a consulting business

Did you pick d? You're on the right track! The problem is phrased to include potential solutions and timeframe. The actions are "explore" and "decide."

When phrasing the problem, think of "START NOW." Besides creating a sense of urgency, this acronym reminds you to ask and answer these questions:

- **Specific:**

  What is the specific problem you want to work on? You can have more than one chart going at a time, but each one should be a defined problem with a specific solution.

- **Timeframe:**

  What is the time when you need to have made the changes? For example, "Find a new job within 3 months." Open-ended tasks linger and goals languish without deadlines.

- **Actionable and appreciable:**

  Can you do this (as opposed to daydreaming) and can you do it so you have appreciable successes? Can you observe and measure results? Example: Suppose you need to take up golf to increase your presence in the business world. You might meet mentors and influencers on the golf course, but you've never played. You set the goal of becoming proficient in golf by the end of the year. You can measure your progress with a chart for recording holes-in-one, par, etc.

- **Realistic:**

  Using the example with golf, what if you phrased the problem as "Win the PGA tournament by the end of next year"? Given your current neophyte status, that is daydreaming, not a solvable problem.

- **Thrilling:**

  Have you phrased the problem so you are excited to get going? The greater your desire to make changes, the more motivated you are to follow your Personal Power Roadmap. Can you say it with eagerness and passion, such as "Get good at golf by the end of next year so I can mingle with movers and shakers and find a great mentor."

- **Now:**

  Are you ready? Now is the time to get going. "Start learning this week how to play golf so I am proficient by the end of the year and can mingle with movers and shakers and find a great mentor."

- **Open**:

  Are you open to doing this, so you will invest the time, energy and resources to reach your proposed solution? "Start learning this week with a top-flight instructor how to play golf so I am proficient by the end of the year and can mingle with movers and shakers and find a great mentor."

- **Workable**:

  Do you have the resources, the time, energy, and money to invest in the solution? No sense in taking up golfing if you are broke and can't pay to get onto the green, much less buy or rent the equipment.

The Personal Power Roadmap must have a doable objective, with specific actions and dates, so cramming everything into one "life plan" invites failure. Understand the importance of focus. Think of "what," "when," "why," "how."

Step 2: Write Your Reasons For and Against; Include Roadblocks and Opportunity Cost

This is like a "pros and cons" list, but more detailed. If we do not know our "why" we can lose our way. "Whys" motivate us. They are the reasons we want to change. We also have reasons we don't want to change. These may be rational ones, or irrational ones, such as fears, doubts, or sad stories. You need to know them both. By writing this out, your desires are more concrete and your fears less threatening. You also need to consider the loss of potential gain from other alternatives when one alternative is chosen. This is the "opportunity cost."

Whenever you make a choice or decision, what you did not choose is lost, and costs you something. If you use the standard "pros and cons" list, you may miss this cost. You may also fail to appreciate the roadblocks and obstacles that lay ahead. Consider, too, your core values and priorities. It's hard to do things that go against your inner grain or you don't care about. You need to care to put the energy, time, and money required to succeed at what you're doing. Ask yourself, what do you personally find meaningful?

When working on this part of the Personal Power Roadmap, think of "PC ROC":

- Pros
- Cons
- Roadblocks
- Opportunity Cost
- Core Values & Priorities

The way you phrase the problem predicts the outcome of your problem solving. If a problem is put in a way it can't be solved, or would be difficult to solve, you won't have much success.

Suppose you need to lose 100 pounds and are not a candidate for gastric bypass. You know that you will have to diet and exercise to lose that weight. So if you approach the problem like this: "It will take forever to lose 100 pounds!" Or "How can I lose that much weight when I can't even lose 20 pounds without suffering?" you are limiting the possibility of success.

What if you put it like this? "I will lose 10 pounds by the end of next month." Even better, "I will lose 10 pounds by the end of next month by eating sensibly and exercising regularly." You are already suggesting solutions. The first is to set a small, easy to attain goal, and the second is to acknowledge that it will require positive actions (eating sensibly and exercising regularly) that will ensure success ("I will lose the weight").

Step 3: Write What You Imagine For the Future

In Chapter 4, you will practice the technique of time travel. You will develop a vision for the future using an exercise that takes you into the future and then back to the past. For now, focus on what you would like to see evolve from your efforts to solve this problem and create change. A strong vision will inspire you to work through the hard parts.

Step 4: Research Your Options, Then Study Them; Use an Effective Method for Storing Your Research

Many problems need knowledge before you can decide the best way to solve them. To make a career change, you'd research job markets and schools. Thinking of moving to a distant location? You'd want to know a lot before leaving. In this part of the Personal Power Roadmap you list or link your research and analysis. This is an objective process, the easiest part to do.

Store your research so it is handy later. In Chapter 5 I discuss storage in more detail. I recommend Evernote for this and other purposes. If you are working on paper, use a tabbed binder, an accordion file, or a file box.

Sources of knowledge are not limited to what you search for online or at the library. Ask questions of others. Many people are eager to give helpful advice if you approach them the right way. Google "how to ask for advice" for how to do this effectively.

Use lateral thinking to connect ideas: In 1968, Dr. Spencer Silver, a scientist at 3M, accidentally discovered a low-tack adhesive. It took six years before a colleague, Art Fry, came up with an idea how to use the adhesive: as a movable bookmark in his hymnal. Some years later, after persistent efforts by some other 3M employees, the Post-it was born.

If we encourage lateral thinking – connecting seemingly disconnected ideas –we can come up with new ideas and inventions. If you want proof of this, Google "inventions by accident." Try the methods in Chapter 5 to come up with novel problem-solving ideas.

Have in mind a problem you need to solve, and opportunities may appear not by magic, but because you connect the problem with something you experience. For example, I wanted to train nasturtiums up the side of my house. I saw an antique coil box spring frame at a junk yard. I attached it to the house and soon the nasturtiums covered the wall. One day I discovered a sparrow's nest in one of the coils. For me this was a much better solution than an ordinary trellis, as I got double duty – flowers and a nest.

Step 5: Have a Plan B for Falling Back or Back Up

The best Personal Power Roadmap also has a "Plan B" built in, so have a viable option in mind. Is there another way to get where you want to go if your first choice fails? You may need to pursue two approaches with one or the other as a backup or "Plan B."

Think of Plan B as your bridge back. If you quit your job to start your own business and your plans don't work out, what is your bridge back to being an employee? Did you burn your bridges by leaving with unpleasant words? Or did you express your gratitude for all that you learned at your last job?

Have you upgraded your skills through courses or experience while working at your own business? Have you kept in contact with others who might help you? Have you done anything to help them? *This is your bridge back, so build it into your plans.*

Having a designated Plan B also has a calming effect. It is your exit strategy in case you need one.

Step 6: Figure Out What You Must Do First: Make it Doable and Bite-Sized

You need to make small, doable tasks. A big problem is a project, and projects must be made into tasks with timelines. You cannot solve every problem at once. Prioritize and focus on what you can do now. Create an action list. This is your itinerary, where you go and when.

If the project is big, you may need more than one Personal Power Roadmap. Suppose you are remodeling your house. The kitchen project needs its own Roadmap. Smaller projects with fewer moving parts can go on another Roadmap.

Do you know the proverb, "Nothing succeeds like success"? Success breeds further success. It inspires new effort. If you make your actions bite-sized and doable, you have something to appreciate and congratulate yourself for achieving.

Suppose you need to lose 40 pounds. This seems daunting, so you put off starting a diet and exercise program. You are planning to go to a special event next month, so you tell yourself this will wreck your diet so wait till it's over. With this approach, you remain 40 pounds overweight.

Suppose you set the goal of losing 5 pounds? That will require far less effort and can be done fairly quickly. After you lose the 5 pounds, you know you can lose weight. You challenge yourself to lose another 5 pounds.

Avoid vague and vast tasks -- that guarantees failure. Suppose your problem is buying a house. You defined it as "buy house by June 1," wrote the reasons this makes sense and the obstacles you face. Then you researched and did a market analysis. You listed your first step: "Review current listings and open houses." You soon exhausted yourself searching online and driving around.

What if you made the first step, "create a checklist of 5 non-negotiables"? You make a list of absolute must-haves: the city/neighborhood, the size, the cost, the proximity to services, whatever you must have or no deal. You can then eliminate all the properties that do not fit your list. Better yet, give this list to a Realtor. Let someone else do the searching. The clearer your Personal Power Roadmap is, the better it works to get you where you want to go.

So now you have your next action, and just doing this makes you much calmer. You can focus on this task, set a deadline and move forward.

Step 7: Keep a Travel Diary: the Log Tracks Progress and Identifies Obstacles

The log is where you list what you did. It tracks progress toward your goal. If you make recording your progress a daily or at least weekly habit, the log will motivate you to continue. It also helps control anxiety: it gives you something to do and proof you are doing something.

The log shows what you are not doing. If you didn't do an item on your action list, why not? Check your Reasons section. Have the reasons changed? Is a "pro" now a "con"? Or did something you listed as a potential roadblock manifest?

The log will show your side trips. This is where you departed from the itinerary (action list). Why? Was it necessary? Did you learn something useful to solving the problem you defined? Or were you procrastinating?

If you are working with others, you can share access to the Roadmap as a whole or in parts by using a shared notebook on Evernote, or shared folders on Dropbox, Google Drive, OneDrive, etc.

Visit the log frequently. Make notes. Put on your calendar a meeting with yourself to go over your Personal Power Roadmap. Assess progress, roadblocks, whether to change the plan based on experience. The Roadmap must be flexible, like one you would take on an actual road trip. If the road is washed out or there is a detour or accident, you need to drive around it. For effective problem solving, you need a living document, not something set in concrete.

If you are stuck, the reason may be somewhere in the Roadmap. If you still are stuck, go to Chapter 7, "Get Unstuck and Get Going Again."

Exercise for Chapter 2

This next exercise will help you focus on now and block out the noise in your mind and the fears, doubts, and negative thoughts that block effective problem solving. To begin, think of yourself as a horse wearing blinders, moving through traffic without distraction.

Exercise 2-1: Unexpected Loss of Job

Imagine this: You just learned your company was sold and your department will be redundant. So your goal is to find a new job or start your own business.

If you focus just on the goal, you may feel overwhelmed with fear, anger, or other negative feelings that can hinder effective action. So focus first on being calm.

Step 1: Use the first essential skill, imagination, to create a calming image, or play music you find soothing or energizing, depending on what you have to do next.

Step 2: Next, use the second essential skill, cognition: write what you want to achieve. Will you seek another job like the one you are losing? Change careers? Open your own business? Take a long overdue vacation and cope with this later? Write the next step. Can that step be broken into smaller steps? Your goal is to find the smallest action you need to do next. In Chapter 5, you will learn specific techniques to encourage objective and creative thinking. For now, jot down whatever comes to mind.

Step 3: Focus on motivation, the third essential skill. Are you feeling charged up? Do you see this sudden problem as a calamity or an opportunity for change? Are you closing down, or opening up? In Chapter 6 you will learn specific techniques for supercharging your motivation. For now, find something that creates a sense of urgency, such as the need to pay your bills, to give you drive.

Don't worry at this point about a complete or detailed Roadmap. This is just an exercise on using the 3 Essential Skills when a problem presents itself. We will return to this imagined problem when we create the Personal Power Roadmap in the next chapter.

Key Points in This Chapter

You can learn the methods and habits of successful problem solvers. Start with a solvable problem. Focus on the present. The Personal Power Roadmap is a valuable, go-to multi tool, fundamental to your success. Using the 3 Essential Skills, follow the 7 Steps to working with the Personal Power Roadmap, beginning with the START NOW questions.

What You Will Learn In the Next Chapter

In the next chapter, "The Power of the Roadmap Chart," we will apply START NOW to an actual problem I faced years ago. You will see what a Roadmap looks like, what formats are available and how to store your Roadmaps. You will learn how to use the Personal Power Roadmap to plan and track effective decision making, problem solving, goal setting, and project creation.

3

The Power of the Roadmap Chart

Case History: Losing a Job

In 1982, I was in the real-life company-sold-need-to-scramble exercise described in Chapter 2. As soon as I heard the news, I rushed to my office and made a list of what to do next. I listed my contacts who might know of job openings. I made calls and sent out resumes.

I reconsidered whether to open my own law practice after one of the executives I worked with encouraged me to hang out my shingle. I had many "reasons" not to do that, including fear of failure and poverty, fear of the unknown. But I did not want another corporate job, so within days of the news, I had put together a business plan, secured a promise of funding, and was looking for an office.

What helped me the most was focusing on the problem instead of avoiding it. The other great lesson was the Roadmap. We did not have computers then. I put hanging folders in a file box with labels such as "Ideas" and "Contacts." I kept a log of everything I was doing. When I felt discouraged, I'd look at the log or sort through the Ideas folder. Keeping the box in order calmed me down. I could take it out of the car wherever I was and work on it. For several months it was my portable office.

I later taught clients how to set up a "business in a box" and even set up two other small businesses using this method. Today you can do this on your phone or your iPad. If I were doing this now, I'd use Evernote to keep everything organized.

Look at the Personal Power Roadmap chart. You will see how you can list reasons for and against, and note potential roadblocks. You can also assess the opportunity cost. If I had the Roadmap chart back then, it would look something like this:

My Personal Power Roadmap for Changing Career Direction

Problem[1] START NOW	Open my own law practice in San Francisco by 4/1/1982	
Reasons[2]	Pros	Cons
	I don't want another corporate job	Money: I don't want to lose my house

	I don't want to work for another horrible boss or company.	San Francisco is one of the most congested legal markets
	I want to be my own boss.	I don't have a sales personality
	Bob thought I would be a big success with my own practice	I am not the rain-maker type
	Other people think so too.	I am not outgoing enough
	I already am getting referrals.	I don't play golf or mingle at clubs
	I will sink or swim according to my level of competence.	I am not good at working the room
	If worse comes to worse, I can look for a regular job.	
	"There's room for one more": it worked when I moved to San Francisco	

	Potential Roadblocks & Opportunity Cost	**Core Values & Priorities**
	My negativity	I care more about practicing law ethically and being of service than making lots of money.
	Lack of self-confidence	My own practice will assure my independence to pursue my values.
	Congested legal market	I care about having time for creative activities and my other interests.

		With a regular job, I will be overloaded with work and have little energy for other areas of my life.
	During the time I am getting up and running, I am losing salary I could earn in a regular job. Can I make this up eventually?	
	I will invest a lot of time and frustration pursuing this. Is it worth it or will I be as miserable in my own practice as I would be in a salaried job?	
	Investing time and money in my own business will have a better payoff eventually, and I will have job security.	
What I imagine for the future	In two years, I will make more than my corporate job pays. I will have satisfied clients referring others. I will get referrals from other professionals. I will swim!	

Research & Analysis[3]	**Research**	**Analysis**
	I read two books on how to open your own law practice.	They both said it was doable and gave similar advice.
	I talked to several people to get feedback, information	
	I checked out rents in San Francisco	I need to examine whether I should share space and work in exchange for rent.

Plan B[4]	Get a regular job if I can't make a go of it

Next Actions[5]	To Do		Due Date
	☐ Find an office in downtown or Civic Center		
	☐ Explore option to do some work in exchange for rent		
	☐ Get cards and stationery when I have address & phone numbers		
	☐ Get office furniture		
	☐ Go to meetings and hand out cards		
	☐ Call contacts to let them know I am available for work		
	☐ Sign up with Lawyer Referral Service		
	☐ Get a Yellow Pages ad if budget permits		
Progress Log	**Date**	**What I did to advance solution/change**	Notes
		[I am writing this in 2015, not 1982, so I do not have my old calendar or progress log from my business-in-a-box]	

Specific Features of the Roadmap Chart

The Roadmap is in seven parts. Each corresponds to a step you need to take. It lets you know what, why, when, how. The first section is where you define or phrase the problem so it is solvable. If it's a decision, or a goal, or a project, the process is the same. We went through the seven steps in Chapter 2. Reminders are written into the chart, so even if the book is not at hand, you can work on your Roadmap.

Whether you work on an electronic device or on paper, whether you store the Roadmap chart online, or in a binder or other container, you follow the same process when filling in the chart.

The Roadmap chart is your fast pass. You don't have to slow down to figure out what to do next. You already know and can just get on with it.

How to Get and Store the Personal Power Roadmap Charts

The Personal Power Roadmap chart is available in four formats: MS Word, PDF, mind map (XMind), and Evernote template. Download them from this website: www.personalpowerroadmap.com/templates You are welcome to make your own in other formats or to customize it for your personal use.

For detailed instructions on how to install and use the Personal Power Roadmap with Evernote, go to: www.personalpowerroadmap.com/evernote-ppr. You will also find tips and tricks for organizing your research in Evernote and how to use the Roadmap chart in separate sections. In Chapter 5, you'll find screenshots of how I used Evernote to organize the research for a project involving relocating to Dubai.

Store your Personal Power Roadmaps for later use. Studying a past one when devising a new Roadmap helps avoid past problems. See it as a study guide, a learning tool.

Action Step: Road Test the Personal Power Roadmap with a Real-Life Scenario

Try out the chart with a personal problem, decision, goal or project. Look at the filled-in sample above to learn how to use this valuable tool if you are having problems creating your Roadmap.

Using the Roadmap to Make a Decision

Case History: Deciding on a Career Change

In the real-life scenario described above, I quickly realized the best option was establishing my own law practice. I will tell you how I reached that decision, and also show you how to use the Roadmap as a decision making tool.

On that day in early 1982 when I heard the company was sold, I had no thought of starting my own practice. I had ruled that out before, after looking for a partner without success. I never considered a solo practice. After running to my office, I made a list of contacts. One was Anne, the secretary to the general counsel of a big company I thought would be a good fit. I sat next to her at a luncheon a few months earlier. She was delighted by my call and said, "Get your resume over here fast

– we just got authorized to hire more attorneys." We agreed to meet in a few days for lunch.

At that lunch, Anne said she was eager for me to work there as I appreciated that secretaries were as important as attorneys in getting work done, that I treated them with respect and believed in women's rights.

Anne told me about a young attorney brought in from a private firm who made a lot of waves. He expected his secretary to do his laundry. When Anne approached him about this, his response was that he had to have a secretary do his laundry because he wasn't married. Anne also told me that her boss had aged 10 years in the last year and his hands were shaking.

I was no longer excited about working for this company. I had been in this situation before and could read the writing on the wall. I figured the young attorney was brought in to do a hatchet job and get rid of the General Counsel and take his place. That night I paced my kitchen and talked to the walls. I didn't want another corporate job where a bloodbath was about to occur. I didn't want to work for someone who gives his laundry to his secretary. How would I know this wouldn't happen no matter where I went?

I revisited the idea of my own law practice. Why did I need a partner? I had assumed that I needed one because I didn't believe I was good at drawing in clients. My partner would be the one who would do the "rain making" while I stayed in the office and did the actual legal work.

As I thought about this, I realized I did not want a partner. I'd heard too many horror stories in my seven-and-a-half years of practice. "He travels the fastest who travels alone" came to

mind. I started to think about being a solo practitioner. I decided to give it a try. The worst that could happen was I would fail and then I would look for a salaried job. I figured I would sink or swim according to my level of competence.

If I had invented the Personal Power Roadmap back then, instead of pacing in the kitchen, I would have written in the first section, "Decide within the next month whether to start my own law practice as a solo practitioner, or whether to seek a salaried job." The rest of it would look much the same as the example above.

Once I decided to start my own practice, I kept busy with my business-in-a-box, which was the predecessor of the Personal Power Roadmap. It contained a logistics folder where I kept track of my activities.

There were moments of sheer panic as I thought about being out there without a paycheck, but I knew I needed to focus on what I had to do next and not get distracted by negative thoughts. I put my horse blinders on, just as we did in Chapter 2. I focused on the task I had to do next. I gave myself pep talks and recited aphorisms (more on that in Chapter 6).

Within a few days of reaching the decision to open my own practice, I received two referrals of business. It calmed me down to know people wanted to be my clients. I saw the path through the woods, and I reminded myself that a journey of a thousand miles begins with a single step.

Using the Roadmap to Set Goals

The START NOW questions work for setting and achieving goals. Those vague New Year's resolutions can "get legs" and run. Go back to the method in Chapter 2 and don't forget to include the PC ROC questions.

I shared the story of how a big problem changed my life. I was thrown into a crisis and had to act quickly, as often happens in life. Now let's look at a situation where there is no crisis and plenty of time to prepare. It involves a goal, and the Roadmap works just as well for goal setting as it does for decision making and problem solving. It doesn't matter if there's a crisis or if there's a slow time to react or to plan.

Case History: Finding the Ideal Mate: From Fantasy to Reality

Elaine was a Multidimensional Problem Solving^{sm} student who wanted to find a husband. She had had disappointing experiences with men she met at the massage parlor where she worked. Even though this was not one of those places that offered sexual massage, the men she met there expected her to cater to their needs and focus on them the way she had when they met her at work. Such lopsided relationships rarely work. But I kept my thoughts to myself and asked her to do an imagination exercise. She was to do this at home, write down everything that she saw when she thought of what she was looking for in a husband. She was to use all her senses and describe the relationship in detail. We would go over it at the next session. It is basically the exercise we did in Chapter 1, Exercise 1-5: Happiness.

The following week Elaine presented me with her notes. In her fantasy, she was walking on a tropical beach with her man. She wore a sarong and he wore a bathing suit. This man doted on her. He adored her, the sun rose and set with her. There was only this vacation scene. The man was a stick figure. There was no description of his personality, values, interests, or lifestyle.

I asked Elaine to answer these questions:

1.   What steps do you need to take to bring about what you imagined?

2.   What would you need to change? Include your attitude. Be specific (e.g., "I need to have a more balanced view of what a relationship involves.").

3.   Are you willing to put time and effort into reaching your vision of happiness?

4.   What change in your present life would make the most difference to achieving your vision?

Elaine had created a lopsided relationship, like what she was experiencing with men she met at work. Only this time she was the one expecting the other to cater solely to her needs. They were in a fantasyland together, some place where one vacations rather than lives. There were no responsibilities, no house to care for or children to raise.

I asked Elaine to focus on where she would meet this man. What places would she go to? What courses might she take that would bring her in contact with the man of her dreams? Would she join clubs or interest groups to expand access to men of substance? Maybe volunteer somewhere?

The following is what the notes for the Roadmap would look like if Elaine followed the Personal Power Roadmap process:

Goal: Meet an eligible bachelor interested in a committed relationship by the end of [insert date three months later]

Reasons: Pros: I need to meet men outside of the workplace.

What I imagine for the future: I settle down with Mr. Right in the suburbs and have one or two children. I have a massage studio at home or nearby so I can work part time and earn my own "mad money."

Research: get adult courses catalog and find two courses where the man I am interested in might study. Join a local church where there are eligible men in the congregation. Find a volunteer organization where the man I am looking for would also volunteer. Sign up for Sierra Club hikes. Stay out of bars and nightclubs. I don't want to meet a barfly.

The first thing to do: create a detailed list of what I am looking for with five non-negotiables so I don't waste time with the wrong men:

> 1. No drinkers, drug takers, womanizers, deadbeats.
>
> 2. Must be clean cut and healthy.
>
> 3. Must be fiscally responsible, a good provider.
>
> 4. Must care about family commitments.
>
> 5. Would be a kind and patient daddy.

By now I think you see how useful the Personal Power Roadmap approach is to decision making, problem solving, and goal setting. It forces you to focus on what you need to do next. It gives you precise tools to figure out how to phrase your problem, decision, or goal. You create steps that will take you where you want to go. The section for progress and notes is a built-in tracking device that keeps you on course.

Using the Roadmap to Create Projects

Complex projects involving teams of people call for specialized software. For smaller projects, the Personal Power Roadmap has room for everything you need. In Chapter 8 you'll find examples of its use with a business project, a decluttering project, and a relationship problem.

As with other uses, you use START NOW to explore your concept and create a solvable problem. The specifics of the project – at a minimum the purpose and time frame – can go in the first section. For example, in Chapter 2 there was a problem involving learning golf. If it were cast as a project, the Problem section of the Roadmap might read: "Get good at golf by the end of next year so I can mingle with movers and shakers and find a great mentor." Seeing the purpose and time frame every time you look at your Roadmap reinforces the "why" of what you are doing, as well as the due date.

Key Points in This Chapter

The Roadmap is an essential tool for creating change in your life. The Roadmap is not just for "problems": Use START NOW with the Roadmap to plan and track effective decision making, problem solving, goal setting, and project creation.

What You Will Learn In the Next Chapter

In the next chapter, "Imagine That! Imagination is the First Essential Skill," you will begin Part Two (The 3 Essential Skills Plus the Personal Power Roadmap Equal Success) You already know how to use the first Essential Skill but will practice honing it with four techniques with variations. You will imagine yourself in a future time and place so you can use that image to design your Roadmap. You will practice how to know it, see it and believe it, to find out what you *really* want.

PART TWO

THE 3 ESSENTIAL SKILLS PLUS THE PERSONAL POWER ROADMAP EQUAL SUCCESS

4

Imagine That! Imagination Is the First Essential Skill

"Imagination is more important than knowledge. For knowledge is limited, whereas imagination embraces the entire world, stimulating progress, giving birth to evolution." – Albert Einstein

You have been using this skill since you were an infant. Even if you don't remember what you were like as a child, just hang out with some children and you will enter the magical realm of imagination.

Imagination is the ability to create a mental image. It's the unconscious mind at work and play. We are born with this essential skill, yet few realize its full potential. In this chapter, we explore ways to maximize our inborn imaginative ability. When you hone this skill, you find solutions to problems and create desired change.

Using imagination, you can break free from linear thinking and encourage related or unrelated ideas to emerge from the unconscious mind. In the first two chapters, you practiced imagining scenes and experiences. You can decide when and where to use this skill, rather than wait for your imagination to kick in randomly.

When Honing Your Imagination, Engage All Your Senses

Have you noticed how particular smells bring back memories? Maybe you pass a bakery and smell spices you associate with Christmas gingerbread. Memories float in as the smell pulls a vision from the unconscious into the conscious mind. Or you are in an elevator with a stranger who is wearing a scent that evokes memories of a lost love. Sounds have the same effect. You hear a song from high school and are taken back to the teen years. On a cold winter day you look at a picture of a beach and imagine lolling on the sands, listening to the waves and feeling the sun warming you. Maybe something you touch or feel triggers your imagination. Have you felt a warm breeze, then thought of a paradise you visited?

Then there's taste. Have you tried an unusual cheese and imagined it melted on toast? Or tried pumpkin ice cream and remembered a distant Thanksgiving?

Let Your Imagination Run Away!

Did you hear this growing up: "Don't let your imagination run away with you"? Does your Inner Parent or Schoolteacher rein you in when you think big? I say, do the opposite! Think big and give free rein to your imagination. Let the second essential skill, cognition, do any necessary "reining."

Stifling imagination stifles creativity and impedes problem solving. If we could just figure everything out using cognition, we'd limit ourselves to what we know or could find by research. What if Einstein had not imagined something beyond what science had proved? Or if Steve Jobs limited himself to what others knew and thought? You wouldn't be using a smartphone.

You can't turn off your imagination, so why not let it suggest new ideas or new ways of viewing your life?

Imagination lets you see what is possible. It's essential to designing the Personal Power Roadmap that takes you where you want to go. You can use it to find where that really is. Even if you think you already know what you want, let's do an exercise that will let you know what that *really* is:

Use Imagination to Change Your Life: Exercise 4-1:

Write what you want to change in your life. You are contemplating changing careers and have identified a new occupation. Or you are planning to move to another town, or making another big life change.

Now sit or lie down in a quiet place. Turn off the phone or notification sounds on your computer. Shut your eyes and see yourself at the new job, the new location, or other life change. Develop the senses: What do you see? What sounds do you imagine? What do you smell, taste and feel in this place?

After you develop this mental image of yourself at a future time and place, examine your emotions:

- **Are you happy?**
- **Is this what you want?**
- **Do you see yourself there, loving your life?**
- **Or was this someone else's vision?**
- **Or your idea based on "rational" factors such as money, or what you thought you should want?**

Next, imagine it's 10 years from now and you are reading what you wrote today after doing this exercise. What would you realize looking back?

- **Did you get where you thought you wanted to go?**
- **Did you stay there?**
- **Did you abandon the dream?**

A journal helps you keep track of your goals. It creates a memory bank. It lets you download negativity. Excuses, regrets, dark imaginings, happenings from those days the Dalai Lama said do not exist on the calendar – yesterday and tomorrow. Keeping the journal is a way to keep track of your Roadmap. You can record your progress on the Personal Power Roadmap or in your journal.

I promised you earlier that you will learn several easy ways to use imagination to know it, see it and believe it, even if your conscious mind does not yet know it. You just learned the first technique, Time Travel, in the life-changing exercise.

Techniques to Hone Imagination

Time Travel Technique: Looking Forward, Looking Backward

This technique puts you in a time other than now. Its purpose is to create a vision of how you would like to be if you solved your current problem and brought about the changes you desire.

> The first part is to look forward in your imagination. What are you doing 10 years from now? You can use another time frame that makes more sense, such as five years or 20 years or even one year. The idea is to visualize what you would like to see as the outcome.

> Write what you envisioned. Put in details. Use the five senses. Take the time to write up a thorough account of your visit to the future.

> Now you will look back at the same time you used when looking forward (5 years, 10 years, whatever time frame you picked). Looking back at yourself as you are now,

> What do you see in your mind's eye?

> What advice would allow you in the present moment to bring about the vision you had looking forward?

How could it help you with the Roadmap you created for this problem?

Write everything you see in your mind's eye.

Some Variations on the Time Travel Technique:

1. A door is opening:

You are in a house that seems familiar. It's not your house, but you are comfortable visiting this house. You know this door opens into a room containing something that will help with the problem you defined. Go into the room and find what that is. It may not be the first thing you find so stay in the room for 10 minutes and find everything it offers. Open closets and drawers. Explore the bookshelf in the room. Look out the window. Note everything: the unconscious mind is revealing important ideas.

2. Train Station:

Imagine you are at the train station, awaiting the next train.

Who is on that train? What will that person tell you that will help you with your problem?

3. A Helpful Gift:

Imagine that person has brought you a gift that will help with your problem.

What is this gift?

You have experienced the power of visualization. You are always doing this, whether imagining what you'll have for dinner or daydreaming or mentally rummaging through your closet to find an outfit for a special event. You do this naturally, without thinking. Imagine how useful this is if you enlist it to work for you to find solutions to the problem you defined for your Roadmap.

Two Techniques to Bypass the Conscious Censor

If you give yourself permission to imagine what you think would make you happier with your life, you can bypass the negative thoughts and limiting beliefs that are the bane of problem solving.

Do you remember the magic fairies of childhood? Tinker Bell could fly. She had a magic wand. I would fly with her to delightful places, spin in the air, and imagine her magical world until I had to return to mundane existence when called to come down to dinner.

I loved Peter Pan, another daydream companion. Peter didn't have to grow up. He could fly, like fairies. He didn't have to do homework or help with the dishes.

We grew up. Our fantasies changed. But the ability to imagine other realms remains. Now you can harness that ability to imagine change and create solutions to problems, make decisions, or set goals.

1. Create a Magic Box

My friend Sherry is an artist. She doesn't write out her problems or makes lists. She believes that what she wants and needs will manifest if she opens an intuitive channel in her mind. She created a magic box to hold her wishes. She imagines they will come true by a date she assigns.

Sherry found the box in an art museum gift shop. Covered with an 18th-century painting of roses and peonies, it held a china cup with the same painting on it. Sherry put a picture of the box on her refrigerator and uses it as the wallpaper on her smartphone. She drinks her morning coffee from the cup and remembers what the box now holds: slips of paper on which she has written what she wants to manifest, such as "sell more paintings." She puts a date on each paper, so her mind is focused on achieving the result in that timeframe. Now she is in receiving mode, and able to spot opportunities to solve her problems and create change.

2. Let Words or Images Trigger Imaginative Solutions

Another friend is a graphics designer. To start his creative process, Bob uses word triggers he finds in the thesaurus and in current culture. He starts with words that relate to the problem he is trying to solve, then searches for synonyms and antonyms. Sometimes an entire concept may be spurred while thinking about something unrelated – while driving, on a walk or most often before drifting off to sleep. Soon pictures form in his mind. He creates different graphics using the mental images, lets them sit for a while, then refines those and selects the best ones to show his client.

You can Google words that surround your problem or decision. In the exercise where you imagined a vacation, you could Google "tropical beach." Examine the images. Do they prompt your imagination to pursue this vacation idea, or do you see something that turns you off? Maybe the beach evokes a mental picture of how you look in a bathing suit. You decide to Google "visit art museums."

Use Imagination to Boost Motivation, the Third Essential Skill

A similar technique worked for me:

Case History: Losing Weight

I had a collection of beautiful braided belts handmade by an artist, but I hadn't been able to wear them for years after putting on weight around the middle. Determined to slim down, I hung the outfit I wanted to wear on a hanger and put a matching braided belt on it. I imagined myself wearing that belt. This image inspired me to stick with my diet and exercise plan and made it easy to substitute a piece of watermelon for a fattening dessert.

Try connecting your image to another one to boost the third essential skill, motivation. If I created an image of the belt and a piece of watermelon, that would empower me. I could put it on the refrigerator door, the way Sherry reminded herself of her magic box.

Thinking of putting the belt with the outfit relied on cognition, but seeing myself being able to wear it with the outfit relied on imagination. This image increased the motivation to achieve the desired result. So, all 3 Essential Skills worked together to create synergy, with the combined effect greater than the sum of the separate effects.

Technique Using Fantasies to Create Reality

In this technique, you write out your fantasy, without criticism or censure.

> **Put in writing what you want if you can have it any way you want. You suspend the critical mind, the negative thoughts, the "Oh, that's impossible!" thoughts.**

> **When done writing the fantasy, give it a rest for a while. Come back to it later and use the cognitive techniques we discuss in the next chapter. When you are in your conscious analytical mind, you can review and analyze the fantasy, line by line. For now, you want to stay in your imaginative mode and ask yourself:**

> **How could you turn this into reality? What would have to happen?**

> **Are you willing to put the time and effort in?**

Writing our fantasy allows us to explore the differences between what we long for and what we settle for. It highlights unrealistic attitudes and beliefs and disabling thoughts. It shows how we have the power to manifest what we want if we commit to the effort required.

Pulitzer Prize-winning author N. Scott Momaday said, "We are what we imagine. Our very existence consists in our imagination of ourselves. Our best destiny is to imagine, at least, completely, who and what, and that we are. The greatest tragedy that can befall us is to go unimagined."

If we can imagine it, we can do it. Hum R. Kelly's "I Believe I Can Fly" the next time you feel stuck in negativity.

Technique Using a Mind Map or a Tree to Sketch the Problem

A mind map is a diagram to visually organize information. You create it around a single concept, which you draw or write in the center of a blank page. You then add subtopics or floating topics associated with the central topic. These can be images, words, hyperlinks, even sounds. After downloading everything that comes to mind, you look for connections.

You can use the mind map as a standalone visual or generate an outline from it. Some mind map software programs create the outline view with no extra work on your part.

Some people like working on huge sheets of paper. Others prefer to use their computer or notepad or smartphone. There are free programs you can try, like XMind (www.xmind.net). I designed the mind map version of the Personal Power Roadmap in XMind. If you are using another mind mapping software, you can import the XMind template into your program.

The mind map uses both imagination and cognition. I include it in this chapter on imagination as an essential skill because it can help download intuitive ideas from the unconscious mind. It allows you to bypass the conscious censor.

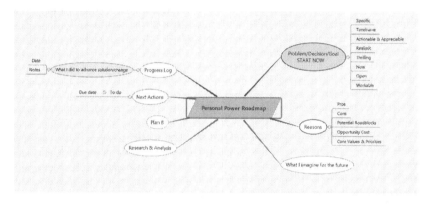

Personal Power Roadmap, Mind Map Format
Download from www.personalpowerroadmap.com/templates

A similar approach is to imagine a tree trunk, linear and bold. This is your problem. Put a label on it. Then imagine branches on your tree. These are the offshoots, or ramifications, of your problem.

Next, imagine leaves on the branches. These are potential solutions to your problem. Don't worry about solving the problem – you are looking for branches and leaves, not "The Right Solution." Gather data now – the branches and leaves – and know that the rest will fall into place at just the right time.

Using What You Imagined in Your Roadmap

Now look at the Roadmap chart you created in Chapter 3. Did you learn anything from trying out these techniques that can help you expand your Roadmap? Look at the sample Roadmap in Chapter 3 where I filled out under "What I imagine for the future," that I saw myself being successful two years later. Why two years? The books I read about opening a solo law practice said it took two years to achieve those results. A friend of mine who read no books got there faster because he had no limiting vision.

Key Points in This Chapter

Imagination is the ability to create a mental image. This skill allows you to break free from linear thinking and encourages related or unrelated ideas to emerge from the unconscious mind. We explored four techniques with variations: time travel, bypassing the conscious censor, using fantasies to create reality, and mind mapping. You imagined yourself in a future time and place so you could use that image to design your Roadmap.

What You Will Learn In the Next Chapter

In Chapter 5, "Figure it Out! Cognition is the Second Essential Skill," you will learn specific techniques to encourage objective thinking and lateral thinking. You will put cognition to work with imagination to craft workable solutions for solving problems and building the life you want. You will get ideas for how to research and store what you need to know for your Personal Power Roadmaps.

5

Figure It Out! Cognition Is the Second Essential Skill

"I did then what I knew how to do. Now that I know better, I do better." – Maya Angelou

A little boy ran up to me in a park and shrieked, "I found gold!" He held out a small rock that glimmered in the sun. He knew what gold was, but he hadn't yet learned about mica. Do you remember the first time you figured something out and had a "Eureka" moment?

Cognition is the ability to use conscious processes to reason, analyze, research, and document our efforts. We are born with this essential skill, yet few realize or harness its potential. In this chapter, we explore ways to maximize our inborn cognitive ability. When you hone this skill, you readily find solutions to problems and create desired change.

Do you know how to use your existing knowledge to generate new knowledge? In this chapter, you will learn techniques to improve your thinking. We will start with some concepts developed by Edward de Bono, a Maltese physician, psychologist, author, and inventor. He originated the term "lateral thinking," wrote the book *Six Thinking Hats*, among scores of books (70) translated into over 30 languages. Considered the world's leading authority on creative thinking, Dr. de Bono has long advocated that "New Thinking" be taught in schools.

We will focus on two of Dr. de Bono's concepts, "Lateral Thinking" and "Six Thinking Hats." Both will help you hone your thinking skills and generate ideas for your Personal Power Roadmaps.

Lateral Thinking in a Nutshell

"Lateral thinking" is creating new perceptions and new concepts instead of following the linear thinking in use since antiquity. Using specific techniques and tools, you can find novel solutions without waiting for inspiration, luck, or random events. By deliberately looking from different angles, you can escape the straitjacket of conventional thinking.

You already tried out some "lateral thinking" approaches without realizing it. In the train station variation of the time travel technique in Chapter 4, you were searching for a different way of looking at things. You opened a new line of thinking by introducing an unconnected idea – a train with someone on it who can tell you something to help you.

In Chapter 4 you also learned about mind mapping as a technique that allows you to generate ideas and bypass the conscious censor. It is also a cognitive tool that encourages lateral thinking.

How to Find New Ideas and Link Seemingly Unrelated Ideas That May Lead to Useful Solutions

"Lateral thinking is made necessary by the limitations of vertical thinking.... The use of lateral thinking is essential in those problem situations where vertical thinking has been unable to provide an answer." (*Lateral Thinking: An Introduction* by Edward de Bono)

Use the following techniques and exercises to develop your ability to think laterally. You will find ideas that extend beyond the ones you already know. You will learn to think creatively, outside the usual box.

Techniques to Hone Cognition

The Six Thinking Hats Technique

One easy-to-grasp method is de Bono's "Six Thinking Hats." Designed for group discussion to help untangle the web of thoughts that cause confusion and frustration, you can do it by yourself or with a friend, or a team at work.

Each hat represents a direction of thinking in which the brain can be challenged. You are separating various thought processes and giving each a chance to have its say. Just rotate through the six hats and write or mind map what you come up with. You can find free "Six Hats" mind maps online at www.biggerplate.com.

Avoid judging, analyzing or drawing conclusions. By compartmentalizing the different thought processes, you may come up with creative solutions. You also provide balance, not using one process while excluding others.

1. **Blue Hat=Define the Focus:** "Thinking about thinking." Here you set up the process and decide what is the subject or goal of the thinking session.

2. **White Hat=Data:** What are the facts? Where can you find data you need (research options). Avoid conclusions or rationalizations.

3. **Red Hat=Emotions:** Intuitive or "gut" feelings. Resist any need to explain or justify your feelings.

4. **Black Hat=Negative Thoughts:** Look for potential problems and faults. Counter Yellow Hat ideas.

5. **Green Hat=Creative:** Be open to all possibilities and alternatives; fantasize about the future.

6. **Yellow Hat=Realistic Optimism:** The values and benefits of a different approach. Logic, not fantasy.

Try Out Six Thinking Hats: Exercise 5-1: Job Offer in Dubai

Imagine this: You are offered a new job in Dubai. You put on the blue hat and decide what to think about. Then the white hat: what data do you have? What do you need to find out? Location, job duties, salary, bonuses, etc.

Now wear the red hat. What are you feeling? What is your immediate reaction? What does your gut tell you?

Next put on the black hat. What negative thoughts come to mind? Contrast this with yellow hat thoughts about career benefits, advantages to living abroad, etc.

What does the green hat tell you? What fantasies are developing as you consider this offer? What if you decline? What happens then?

I did this exercise and created a mind map using XMind. The program is free: www.xmind.net. You can find a free six hats template there: www.xmind.net/m/QPvi/ or on Biggerplate at: www.biggerplate.com/search.aspx .

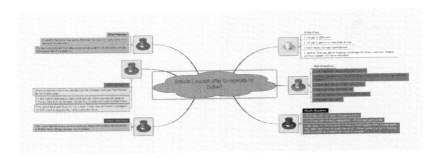

Should I Accept Offer to Relocate to Dubai? Mind Map
For larger image go to www.personalpowerroadmap.com/mind-maps

A key advantage to using the Six Thinking Hats technique is we free ourselves from the dictates of reason and allow intuition to have a voice. It is hard to make decisions, solve problems, or pursue goals when the unconscious mind is opposed to the reasoning mind. Unexpressed doubts and feelings interfere with motivation and produce procrastination.

How Important is Knowledge?

Some years ago my garbage disposal wouldn't work. I called a plumber. He entered the kitchen, quickly stuck a metal tool in the sink and removed it, then turned the switch on to prove the disposal was now unstuck. This took less than a minute. I protested at paying for an entire hour, so he changed washers while he was there. But I was annoyed to learn that my problem only took seconds to fix, at great expense.

I was telling friends about this, and one said she went to a plumbing supply place and bought the tool plumbers use to unstick disposals, so she could fix her disposal herself. Another said she used a broomstick when her disposal got stuck.

A few years later, my disposal wouldn't work. Never having bothered to buy the special tool, and unable to get it working with the tools I had on hand, I called a friend coming over later that day to ask if he had this tool and could bring it along. He wasn't home. At that point, I fetched a broom, stuck it in the disposal, and pushed it against a metal part. It took one light push, and the disposal was no longer "broken."

Isn't it amazing how problems disappear if you know a "secret" easy way, such as the broomstick? I didn't need special tools, expensive experts, or physical strength – just a tip that an ordinary household item could fix the problem.

Now we have so much online, you don't even need to call a friend. Just Google "fix garbage disposal."

The Digital Era Makes Problem Solving Easy

It is easier today than ever before in history to learn. We have the Internet and search engines such as Google, so all kinds of knowledge are a few clicks away. We don't have to spend much time in the School of Hard Knocks, or even the library.

People go to school for years on end nowadays and learn many technical things, but that doesn't mean they've learned how to use their cognitive abilities to cope with the problems of daily living.

I went to a potluck party at the house of a man said to be a member of the Prometheus Society, a "beyond Mensa" organization whose members have the IQ of an Einstein. I read the spines of the books on his bookshelf trying to decipher the general topics. Despite my extensive education, I didn't understood a single one. I guessed astrophysics.

I noticed before entering his house he hadn't bothered to cut the bough of a juniper blocking access to the front door. Guests had to push it aside to get to the door handle. Once inside, I went to the bathroom and discovered it was filthy. The host provided only plastic forks and knives. Someone brought a big pot of soup, but it went uneaten since there were no spoons.

I concluded this man, as brilliant as he was, had a low IQ for daily living. How could he fix this? Try Googling "how to throw a party," for starters.

"If You Can't See The Problem, You Can't Solve The Problem."

Uncle Jack's Steakhouse founder, Willie Degel, likes to say on his popular TV program, Restaurant Stakeout, "If you can't see the problem, you can't solve the problem." He sets up hidden cameras and microphones and then views banks of monitors to see what's going on. He whittles down a large problem to a specific one. The restaurant owner may know that cash is disappearing, but after Willie asks questions, the focus shifts to individual employees. Degel is researching when he monitors the behavior of employees who are not aware they are being observed. The more he knows about what's going on, the more clues on how to solve the problem.

Try out Willie Degel's Approach:

Exercise 5-2: In Front of the Camera: Research and Planning

Imagine you had cameras recording your life. Now analyze the videos.

- What do you see? Make a list of problem areas.
- Ask yourself: What do you need to examine further?
- Where should you focus? Rank the problems so you do next what is essential, not what is easy.

A Movable List: How to Use Evernote

"Daddy!" I called out as my father was getting ready to leave the house. "Will you bring back some ice cream?" I was sick in bed and felt that the least I deserved for my suffering was something cold and creamy. My father took out a little notebook he carried in his coat pocket and wrote down my request.

My father got me into the habit of keeping notes on what I had to do. Today I use Evernote rather than paper, dictating notes on my Evernote smartphone app or using the Clipper on my browser.

I learned in the School of Hard Knocks that what I didn't put down on paper (or later on my computer) was forever lost or found only after a time-consuming search. I also learned that the simple list could be expanded into much more useful charts and logs, which could be saved as templates for later use.

Let's look at some ways to collect, store and mine research and ideas to aid in decision making, problem solving, goal setting, and project creation:

1. File cards: this was how we did it before the Digital Era. They need rubber bands or file boxes, paper clips and other paraphernalia to keep them from scattering.
2. File folders: this was the way I created the "business in a box" I described in Chapter 3.
3. Post-its: an amazing invention, these sticky notes are available in many sizes and shapes, but get stuck in the wrong places.
4. Digital formats: any electronic app or program that allows recording of information. By far the best and most efficient way, because we can manipulate the data and still can print it out on paper, cards, Post-its, etc. If you worry about losing digital data due to a virus or an electromagnetic pulse (EMP) from a nuclear explosion, make copies and bury them in a tin box in your backyard. Don't worry about obsolete storage media or programs: print to PDF to save documents and store in the cloud in protected databases such as Carbonite, iCloud, Dropbox, etc.

How to Make a Roadmap in a Box: Technique

In Chapter 3 I talked about using a box in 1982 when I needed to plan a major change in my life. This was a regular file box in which I hung hanging folders with labels such as "Ideas" and "Contacts." If you really hate using computers, this is still an option. Or if the material you're collecting while researching would be hard to scan or get through the Internet, it might furnish a reason to use a physical folder and files. But there are such better ways to do things with existing technology and programs available on all platforms. Today I would make my box with Evernote.

Take a "banker's box" file box, the kind with indentations on the short sides so you can readily move it around. They are 12 x 10 x 15 inches. If you get this type of box, you can hang legal-sized tabbed file folders in the box as though it were a file drawer. Make tabs that replicate the seven parts of the Roadmap chart:

1. **Problem (or decision, goal, or project)**

2. **Reasons**

3. **What I imagine for the Future (just use "Future")**

4. **Research & Analysis**

5. **Plan B**

6. **Next Actions**

7. **Progress Log**

Put the necessary papers in each folder and go into action. You can carry this box around and work on your Roadmap wherever you are. You don't need a desk or Internet connection, just determination to move forward.

You can also do all this with an accordion folder or a file cabinet.

How to Use Evernote: Technique

While there are many apps and programs to help with research and analysis, my favorite is Evernote. In its simplest use, it functions as a digital file cabinet, where you find stuff using the search engine. With a short learning curve, you can use tags or notebooks and notebook stacks to organize everything. The developers keep adding functions and integrations with popular services such as Dropbox, and like the iPhone, many users are writing tips, tricks, and templates for Evernote.

I provided the Personal Power Roadmap as an Evernote template because more and more I find Evernote to be the easiest way to keep on top of everything. You can save your XMind templates to Evernote (see File menu) and the note contains a direct link back to the mind map and also lists any embedded notes at the bottom of the image. See this screenshot:

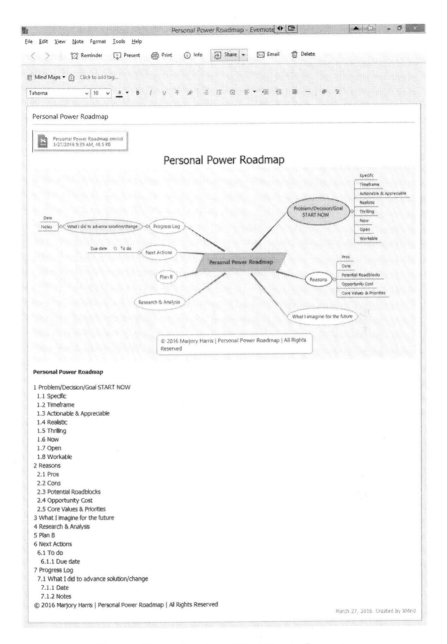

Personal Power Roadmap Mind Map in Evernote
For larger image go to www.personalpowerroadmap.com/evernote-ppr

Evernote is a movable list because it is on every electronic device I use (desktop computer, laptops (Windows and Mac), tablets, phone and online from anywhere).

Evernote is a free cloud-based program that works on all platforms and can be downloaded to your desktop.

If I wanted to convert the "business-in-a-box" file box to Evernote, I would create a notebook stack, then put in notebooks with the same labels I used on the hanging folders in the actual box. Or I might just use one notebook and create a Table of Contents, a function built into the program that puts links on one note to all the notes in the notebook.

Evernote acts as my central clearinghouse, my digital brain. Because it connects to other programs such as Dropbox and Google Calendar, and also to most of the "to do" programs like Nozbe, DropTask, or Asana, it makes record keeping a snap. Much of this book was dictated into Evernote.

Evernote works on all platforms and can also be accessed online if you have none of your own devices with you. For more tips and tricks on using Evernote with your Personal Power Roadmaps, go to: www.personalpowerroadmap.com/evernote-ppr.

I suggest you create a stack of notebooks for the problems you are working on. You can keep your charts in one of the notebooks in your problem stack. If you want this stack to show up at the top of your Notebooks list, just put "!" in front of it. Label one notebook in the stack "Templates." Keep the Evernote template you downloaded from the link in this book in this notebook with any tweaks you made to it. Copy it as needed to other notebooks.

I suggest a notebook for each major problem, decision, project, or life change you are working on. Your Personal Power Roadmap goes in that notebook with research notes, emails you clipped, whatever relates to it. Make a shortcut out of your Personal Power Roadmap note. You can do this by right-clicking on the note and selecting "Add to Shortcuts." Once in the Shortcuts bar, you can drag the item to the position you like. If you no longer need it on the Shortcuts bar, right click and select "Remove from Shortcuts." An example in the next section is based on Exercise 5-1: Job Offer in Dubai.

How to Analyze Your Research and Incorporate it Into Your Personal Power Roadmap: Technique

Let's return to the job offer in Dubai exercise that illustrated using the Six Thinking Hats technique. The mind map raised issues that required research. Under Black Hat thinking, I was concerned that the extra income may go to housing and not be available for travel or savings. I Googled "cost of housing in Dubai" and found a cost-of-living chart I clipped to Evernote using the web clipper extension. I found a few more articles and saved them for later reading. I saved the Google search page in Evernote for later reference. I then Googled "working abroad for your company" and found web pages devoted to the pros and cons of working abroad. I found a Forbes article that gave me a few more things to think about. In less than an hour online I found answers to many of my questions about life in Dubai and the effect on my career of working abroad. I created a table of contents note in Evernote that contained links to these notes:

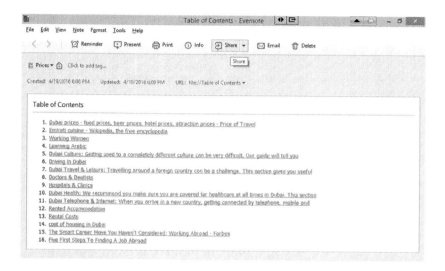

Table of Contents Note in Evernote
For larger image go to www.personalpowerroadmap.com/evernote-ppr

I can reorganize this by topic:

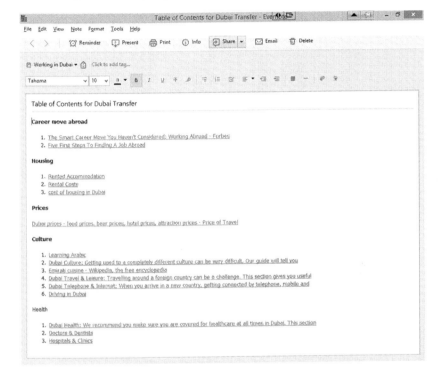

Reorganized Table of Contents Note in Evernote
For larger image go to www.personalpowerroadmap.com/evernote-ppr

As I learn more about Dubai, I can store it in my notebook or just use the "Dubai" tag to find it all later. I can dictate notes on my smartphone and also take pictures. I can set reminders and sync to my Google calendar. I can also email items to and from Evernote.

◢ **Dubai Job Offer**

Culture (4)

Health in Emirates (3)

Housing (3)

Prices (2)

Travel in area (1)

Working in Dubai (5)

Screenshot of Dubai Notebook Stack in Evernote

Dubai Job Offer ▾

Created	Updated	Title	Notebook
11/11/2015 4:09 PM	11/11/2015 4:29 PM	Table of Contents for Dubai Transfer	Working in Dubai
11/11/2015 4:00 PM	11/11/2015 4:00 PM	Dubai prices - food prices, beer prices, hote...	Prices
11/11/2015 3:59 PM	11/11/2015 3:59 PM	Emirati cuisine - Wikipedia, the free encycl...	Culture
11/11/2015 3:58 PM	11/11/2015 3:58 PM	Working Women	Working in Dubai
11/11/2015 3:57 PM	11/11/2015 3:57 PM	Learning Arabic	Culture
11/11/2015 3:57 PM	11/11/2015 3:57 PM	Dubai Culture: Getting used to a completel...	Culture
11/11/2015 3:56 PM	11/11/2015 3:56 PM	Driving in Dubai	Culture
11/11/2015 3:56 PM	11/11/2015 3:56 PM	Dubai Travel & Leisure: Travelling around a...	Travel in area
11/11/2015 3:56 PM	11/11/2015 3:56 PM	Doctors & Dentists	Health in Emirates
11/11/2015 3:56 PM	11/11/2015 3:56 PM	Hospitals & Clinics	Health in Emirates
11/11/2015 3:55 PM	11/11/2015 3:55 PM	Dubai Health: We recommend you make s...	Health in Emirates
11/11/2015 3:55 PM	11/11/2015 3:55 PM	Dubai Telephone & Internet: When you arri...	Prices
11/11/2015 3:55 PM	11/11/2015 3:55 PM	Rented Accommodation	Housing
11/11/2015 3:55 PM	11/11/2015 3:55 PM	Rental Costs	Housing
11/11/2015 3:54 PM	11/11/2015 3:54 PM	cost of housing in Dubai	Housing
11/11/2015 3:54 PM	11/11/2015 3:54 PM	The Smart Career Move You Haven't Consi...	Working in Dubai
11/11/2015 3:54 PM	11/11/2015 3:54 PM	Five First Steps To Finding A Job Abroad	Working in Dubai

Screenshot of Notes in Dubai Job Offer Notebook in Evernote
For larger image go to www.personalpowerroadmap.com/evernote-ppr

To learn Evernote tips and tricks, use free guides you can find by Googling "Evernote tips and tricks." It does not take long to be a ninja user. If you Google "Evernote ninja" you can get there even faster.

To get your research into the Personal Power Roadmap, you can copy and paste the contents or put in a URL link to the online Evernote note. If your Roadmap is already in Evernote, you can copy the note link and paste it into the Roadmap. You may also want to share your Roadmap or the notebook in Evernote, both of which can be done with a few clicks, as easily as emailing.

If your Roadmap is not handy, but you have a sudden brilliant idea, create a note in Evernote (or email to your Evernote account) and insert a check box in front of your note. Later when you take the information in the note and work on that, maybe to incorporate into your Roadmap, check off that box.

Key Points in This Chapter

Cognition is the ability to use conscious processes to reason, analyze, research, and document your efforts. "Lateral thinking" is creating new perceptions and new concepts instead of following the linear thinking in use since antiquity. You can use de Bono's Six Thinking Hats technique to separate the thought processes. By compartmentalizing the different thought processes, you may come up with creative solutions. You can acquire knowledge readily using Internet search engines and store and categorize what you learned in Evernote or in a file box with hanging folders.

What You Will Learn In the Next Chapter

In Chapter 6, "Move Along the Path to Success: Motivation is the Third Essential Skill," you will learn techniques to supercharge your engine so you are energized to get going. You will learn a technique that uses all 3

Essential Skills for creating an instantaneous good habit to achieve success.

6

Move Along the Path to Success: Motivation Is the Third Essential Skill

Diana Nyad, 64 years old, swam the 110-mile passage between Cuba and Florida. For 53 hours she moved through waters infested with venomous jellyfish and sharks before walking ashore in Key West. It was her fifth and last try. Her first attempt was at age 28. At age 30 she stopped swimming and did not resume until age 60. Her motto: "Never, ever give up."

Do you ever wonder why some people have "get up and go" and others don't? Why some move forward in top gear and others creep along in bottom gear? We are all born with the essential skill of motivation. Remember the baby learning to walk? It is our nature to go into action, but as we grow up, we may lose our inborn "get up and go." You will learn more about that in the next chapter, "Get Unstuck and Get Going Again," but here we want to focus on how to increase this essential skill by using the other two skills, imagination and cognition, and some easy-to-do techniques.

Do You Have a Reason to Get Going?

A motive is a reason to get going. It comes from the Latin word "to move." We need to have a reason to take action. For some people, a problem puts them into motion, for many a problem stops them in their tracks. If you don't move quickly to problem solving when confronted with the problem, then you have the problem of how to get motivated, or how to get unstuck.

Some reasons our desire "to do" may diminish are poor health, negative social training, depression, and encouraging pessimistic thoughts by repetition. Nothing kills motivation as fast as telling yourself sad stories, your own or ones you collect. Do you have a history or story of failure? Or is it just now, when confronting a major problem requiring a life change, that you are thinking negatively?

Action Steps

Create an Image

Ask yourself why you want to make the change. Is it because you have to, in the aftermath of losing your job or having a relationship end? What would you like to see happen? Start with a technique you've already learned for honing the imagination skill. Create an image of what it is you want to achieve, or how you want to be. You see yourself looking the way you'd like to look, doing the kind of work you'd like to do, in the relationship you truly want. You get the picture, don't you? Because it is a picture. You're creating a vision of yourself having already become how you'd like to be.

Find a Reason That Sings to You

Do you stop with the first reason that comes to mind? It may not be your reason or one you emotionally connect with. It may be someone else saying, "Get a better job!" or your college buddy tells you how much he makes now, so your inner censor says to you, "You should make more money, so get a better-paid job." You need to find a reason that creates a desire, one you fully support, one consistent with your core values and priorities, not someone else's. Write your reasons until you find one that urges you to act.

Technique: Create an Anchor Image or Word

Use imagination and cognition to create an anchor image to keep you motivated. This will connect a thought or mood to an image. To substitute a better mood and create a new and healthier habit, use an anchor word. For example, if you overeat for consolation because you feel unloved or unwanted, try the Happiness exercise from Chapter 1 and then create a shortcut so you can change your mood with just one quick image or word. Pick a healthy, low-calorie food such as watermelon, and use that word and image when you think of eating a fattening food. Soon it will become an instantaneous habit. When you're thinking "fudge sundae" a desire for watermelon or some other sweet fruit will take its place.

Create an Anchor Image or Word Exercise

Exercise 6-1: Anchor Creation

> Take a habit you want to change and create a word or image of a better habit. Practice associating the bad habit with the image of the better habit.

Look at "Case History: Losing Weight" in Chapter 4 for an example.

More Techniques to Hone Motivation

Six Thinking Hats Technique

> Do the Six Thinking Hats exercise from Chapter 5 and come up with at least three good reasons to get going. Put these on your Personal Power Roadmap. Pay especial attention to the "Core Values & Priorities" section under "Reasons."

If you had earlier completed the "Reasons" section but are now losing momentum, rework the START NOW questions in Step 1. Pay attention to the "PC ROC" under "Reasons" (Pros, Cons, Roadblocks, Opportunity Cost, Core Values & Priorities). You may need to rethink these.

If you have been recording your progress in the Progress Log, look at what you noted, the image of the future, the results of the Six Thinking Hats exercise, and other actions. Does a particular entry (or lack of entries) jar your thinking? Remember, the Personal Power Roadmap is flexible, not cast in concrete. Make whatever changes are necessary to stay on track.

Select a Reward, Treat, or Incentive to Increase Motivation

The next technique for increasing motivation relies on cognition. If you used the Six Thinking Hats method, you now have a list of the reasons that underlie your desire to change. You need to be specific here. To lose weight, you need to state how much and put a time and date on this. Is there some special occasion you want to lose weight for? Do you need to fit into an outfit for an upcoming wedding or something like that? Going to a reunion may motivate you to get on with that goal. These are incentives that will keep you on track.

Rewards, treats or incentives are visions of the future. They function as magnets, pulling you toward your goal.

Visualize yourself already there, being admired for your achievement. Give yourself a reward or treat. You deserve it for your hard work!

Set up a competition with yourself or others. Maybe you just started an exercise program and are planning to enter a marathon, so that keeps you on track. Maybe it's enough of a motivator to keep a log of your exercise, with small, doable goals. When you achieve the first goal, you prove to yourself that

you can do what's required, and it helps you get on with the next step.

Using the technique of research, you may find specific motivations you hadn't thought of. When I Googled "how to get motivated to lose weight" I found information on different websites where people who had already given this much thought provided tips. Again there is no need to reinvent the wheel or to learn this in the School of Hard Knocks. Let Google be your guide.

Affirmations, Aphorisms, Words of Hope, Mantras, or Motivational Quotes

Another way to increase motivation is to use motivational sayings. Whether you call them affirmations, aphorisms, words of hope, mantras or inspirational quotes, repeating these regularly can boost your resolve. If you Google "motivational sayings" you will soon have a big collection. I included below some of my favorites, but I encourage you to create your own list of "words of hope" and to Google whenever you need to mine the quote sites for gold.

Record a motivational mantra and play it every day as you make breakfast or drive to work. You could also put it on your phone as the wallpaper or splash screen. You can attach it to your refrigerator door. This is helpful when trying to lose weight. Put a picture of yourself at a lower weight and some encouraging words such as "Nothing tastes as good as feeling thin feels." We all occasionally hear sayings that perk us up and give us hope. Collect your own powerful words of hope in a little blank book, or in your binder, or in an Evernote notebook. Make it a habit to reprogram your mind with positive sayings.

Here are a few favorites:

"Our greatest weakness lies in giving up. The most certain way to succeed is always to try just one more time." – *Thomas Alva Edison*

"If you're going through hell keep going." – *Winston Churchill*

"Most of the important things in the world have been accomplished by people who have kept on trying when there seemed to be no hope at all." – *Dale Carnegie*

"Inaction breeds doubt and fear. Action breeds confidence and courage. If you want to conquer fear, do not sit home and think about it. Go out and get busy." – *Dale Carnegie*

"A journey of a thousand miles begins with a single step." – *Laozi*. This reminds me that no matter how difficult the going, it is just one step at a time.

Do You Put off Doing Things Until You Are at an Externally Imposed Deadline?

If you rely on stress and pressure for motivation, consider the downside. A friend of mine confessed he is motivated by deadlines. He puts off doing things he doesn't want to do or doesn't like to do until he absolutely has to do them. But isn't there a better way? I know if I don't need to work under pressure, I am less likely to make mistakes. I am also a lot less anxious. I find if I do things in chunks and get little housekeeping things out of the way early, it lessens the stress and motivates me to finish the project without time pressure.

Create a Winning Pep Talk

Be your own cheerleader and give yourself a rousing pep talk. Merriam's defines a pep talk as "a usually brief, intense, and emotional talk designed to influence or encourage an audience." You are the audience and the speaker. Use a mind map program or just a note to create your pep talk. Here is one I created for keeping this book on track:

"I know I can do this! I've done big projects before. It's just a matter of taking one step after another until I get there. I have what it takes. I can do it!"

An inspiring vision can help, like seeing yourself crossing the finish line.

One day a client and I were standing in my garden when we heard a good deal of squawking overhead. She pointed to a baby hawk taking flying lessons. We were transfixed by this fledgling as it made bigger and bigger circles in the sky. The squawking diminished as the bird got more and more confident in its ability to fly. So think of this: a bird keeps flying. Otherwise, it will fall to the ground. It just knows it can fly because it does.

One of my favorite motivational songs is "I Believe I Can Fly." Imagine what you can achieve once you see yourself doing what you imagine.

Inspiring Music (YouTube "Motivational Music")

Create your own marching band to follow. Find and listen to music that inspires you to pick up the pace, "Rocky" type music. If you want free recordings, go to YouTube and look for Bill Conti. He did the themes for the "Rocky" series and "The Right Stuff." Some other favorites:

Rihanna: "Live Your Life"
Shirley Bassey: "My Life"
Frank Sinatra: "I Did It My Way"
"Chariots of Fire"
"I Believe I Can Fly"

Make your own playlist!

Use the Personal Power Roadmap for Goals and Resolutions

Around New Year's, many people feel motivated to make changes. The time-honored tradition of making (and breaking) "New Year's resolutions" fuels TV ads. We feel charged up and vow that next year, we will finally do all the things we've put off doing for years. It isn't too long into January before that feeling fizzles out and we need to recapture that charged-up feeling. In June, we move the bulky exercise machine from our bedroom to storage. Out of sight, out of mind.

Break the habit of breaking New Year's resolutions by using the Personal Power Roadmap to work on a few goals for the coming year. You can organize this in Evernote by using a notebook stack or a note with links to the individual Personal Power Roadmaps you set up. For instructions on how to do this, go to:

www.personalpowerroadmap.com/evernote-ppr.

Key Points in This Chapter

We were all born with the essential skill of motivation. You can increase this by using imagination and cognition. You need a reason that creates a desire, one you fully support, one consistent with your core values and priorities, not someone else's. Rewards, treats or incentives are visions of the future. They function as magnets, pulling you toward your goal. You can gain momentum with pep talks, motivational quotes and music. An anchor image or word uses imagination and cognition to keep you motivated to achieve success.

What You Will Learn In the Next Chapter

In Chapter 7, "Get Unstuck and Get Going Again," you begin Part Three. You will learn how to get going again if you are stuck. You will learn the elements of cognitive therapy – how to overcome negative thoughts, the enemies of effective problem solving and change. You will learn how to remove "malware of the mind," how to end procrastination, and how to get out of the perfectionism trap.

PART THREE

GET UNSTUCK AND GET GOING AGAIN, APPLICATION OF THE 3 ESSENTIAL SKILLS AND THE PERSONAL POWER ROADMAP TO REAL-LIFE CASES, AND THE CHALLENGE OF CHANGE

7

Get Unstuck and Get Going Again

"We've all found ourselves in stuck states, in which we recycle our own mental dirty dishwater." Tony Robbins, *Ultimate Power*

Dump Your "Mental Dirty Dishwater" and Get Out of Your Paper Bag

How do you get rid of the dirty dishwater and get a fresh flow of energy? Start by understanding your "reasons" for getting stuck and how they relate to reality.

Find Out What Keeps You Stuck: Exercise 7-1: Trapped in a Paper Bag

Imagine this: You are inside a giant paper bag. It's dark in there, and getting smelly.

What would you do to get out of this bag? Would you punch a hole? Would you try tearing it with your fingernails? Make the image vivid. Sense the suffocating quality of the air in the bag, that stale smell. Feel how cramped your muscles are in this bag. Create the motivation you need to rip the bag open, or to kick a big hole in it with your foot or your fists. Punch it as much as you want and tear it as much as you want. Get out that sense of frustration that you're stuck in this bag.

Now, see your stuckness as a big paper bag. *You stay in it only because something in your own mind keeps you there.* As soon as you figure out what that is, you can step out of the bag and resume working on your Personal Power Roadmap.

Are You Being Pestered by NATs?

I'm not referring here to "gnats," those annoying little insects that fly around your head when you leave fruit out on the counter to ripen. I'm talking about the ones inside your head. In cognitive behavioral therapy, "Negative Automatic Thoughts" (NATs) cause emotional problems. By identifying our negative thoughts and arguing with them, we can change our moods and our behavior.

The major cause of "stuckness" are these pesky NATs. You might protest, "But I have a sound reason for why my plan isn't working. It's not because of a negative thought but because of [fill in the blank]." Sometimes, events happen beyond your control, such as a family emergency, or an accident requiring recovery time. But when you are stuck, you need to determine whether it's from a negative thought interfering or an actual event beyond your control.

Ask yourself, "If I explain this to someone who is not afraid to tell me what they believe is true, would they say that my excuse is a good one?" If not, consult David Burns's list of common negative thoughts and cognitive distortions or the one I provide later in this chapter:

1. **All or nothing, black or white**: if you are not perfect, then you are a failure.

2. **Overgeneralization:** if one bad thing happened to you, that's proof of a pattern.

3. **Mental filter:** you dwell on the negatives and ignore the positives.

4. **Discounting the positive:** your positive qualities don't count, even if they contradict your actual experience.

5. **Jumping to conclusions:** mind reading and fortune telling: you believe people are thinking badly of you; you can predict the future, and it is bad.

6. **Magnification and minimization:** you catastrophize and awfulize so something is worse than it is. Or you do the opposite: if it is good, you make that insignificant.

7. **Emotional reasoning:** your feelings are your reality. "I feel really stupid, so I am really stupid."

8. **Should statements:** you criticize yourself and others with "shoulds," "musts," and "ought tos." The mother of guilt: "You shouldn't make me feel so unloved" or "I should love myself, but I mustn't because then people will think I'm conceited." A great way to feel guilty, angry, offended, hurt.

9. **Labeling:** a shortcut from labeling an experience to mislabeling yourself: "I broke the cat's feeding dish" becomes "I'm a bumbling idiot."

10. **Personalization:** you are the responsible one when something bad happens. Or you blame others. This combines well with "should statements": "I should have warned her not to take that road, that there are accidents on that stretch, but she should have known that and stayed home."

Adapted from *Feeling Good: The New Mood Therapy* by David D. Burns, M.D.: Copyright ©1980.

Once you identify your NAT, you need to find a more helpful way of thinking about the situation. Pretend you are in court, presenting your case. What evidence supports the NAT? What is against it? Now be the judge and make a ruling. If you come up with "yes, but" thoughts, repeat the process.

Look at these negative thoughts as "malware of the mind" that you need to remove so the operating system can function.

Remove Malware of the Mind: Exercise 7-2:

Imagine this: You are upset with someone, but you cannot tell them that. It may be your boss, a valued client, your partner, or someone else where you know that telling them how you feel will just cause more problems.

Imagine that you may tell them everything you think about them. In a quiet place, where no one can hear you, tell that person what you think and feel. Don't spare anything. Get it all out. You may have to run the program more than once, but you will experience great relief.

I hope you did this with something that's bothering you. Because if you did, you just learned one of the best programs for clearing out malware of the mind: you downloaded the negativity.

Turning Negative Thoughts Into Positive Ones: A Phone Call Interrupts a Fudge Sundae

I was 20 years old, a college student facing a dateless Saturday night. Feeling unloved and unwanted, I made a big bowl of ice cream with fudge sauce. I was tucking into it when the phone rang. A young man had called and invited me to a party. In seconds, I lost my appetite for the fudge sundae. I washed it down the sink, then rummaged through my closet for a party dress. Sadness became elation in an instant.

Our thoughts influence our emotions. When I was sorry for myself, alone on a Saturday night, I had a runaway appetite. The fudge sundae promised a momentary consolation. But the phone call lifted my spirits and killed my appetite.

You don't need to wait for a phone call. You can transmute the negative thoughts into positive ones, and your mood will change.

Cognitive Therapy in a Nutshell

Cognitive therapy was the brain child of a psychoanalyst, Aaron T. Beck. It's an ancient idea. The Greek philosopher Epictetus was quoted: "Nothing else is the cause of anxiety or loss of tranquility except our own opinion." We can change that opinion. The following is a stripped down version that may work for you. It is not meant to replace psychotherapy or medications if your depression or anxiety is beyond the garden-variety sort. If you try these techniques and they don't work, then consider seeking professional help.

1. Note your negative thoughts.
2. Examine the evidence.
3. Argue with the thoughts.
4. Write the thoughts and your arguments in a journal or on the Four Thinking Hats to Explore and Remove Cognitive Distortions mind map you can download from: personalpowerroadmap.com/mind-maps.

If you are not sure what your negative thoughts are, check this short list since most fall into these categories:

1. I'm no good/I'm not good enough/I'm a bad person/I'm a failure
2. I can't do it/it's impossible/it won't work no matter what I do
3. I'll never amount to anything so why try?
4. Nobody cares about me
5. I'm worried that if I change anything, I will fall apart

Mind Map Using Four Thinking Hats Technique to Explore and Remove Cognitive Distortions

Variation on Six Thinking Hats Mind Map
Download from www.personalpowerroadmap.com/mind-maps

This is a variation on the Six Thinking Hats technique from Chapter 5. This one uses the red, black and white hats and one I added, a purple hat representing "should" or guilt-inducing messages. You can download this XMind template from:
personalpowerroadmap.com/mind-maps.

Many problems are rooted in depression or anxiety. It is hard to get going on changing your life when you're feeling depressed or anxious, even if those feelings did not bring about the problem. But often our problems stem from these feelings. If they're not caused by these conditions, then these conditions cause problems when trying to solve problems, make decisions, set goals, or carry out projects.

You don't apply for a job you know you're qualified for. When you think about being interviewed, you get anxious. Or you're depressed and you don't feel motivated right now to do everything you need to do to prepare for a job interview. Why? You haven't bought clothes lately because you gained 20 pounds and don't think you will make a good presentation. So you decide you need to lose the 20 pounds first, get new clothes, and then get interviewed. But you don't get around to losing 20 pounds because you feel so down, and it helps you feel better, at least temporarily, if you eat a pound of chocolates. Put those four hats on and figure out what's going on in your mind. Get out of that 20-pound paper bag and get to the interview!

End Procrastination with the Four Thinking Hats Technique

When we procrastinate, it is because we don't want to do something, or we may want to do it, but we are stopped by the belief we can't do it or that we can't do it well.

Look at this mind map. If procrastination is stopping you from working your Personal Power Roadmap, download this mind map from: personalpowerroadmap.com/mind-maps and test drive it. Save your map to use the next time you get stuck.

Explore Procrastination Mind Map
Download from www.personalpowerroadmap.com/mind-maps

One Step Technique

Ask yourself, what is the one step you could take that would change this problem? Ask yourself how realistic that one step is. If your answer is winning the lottery or Publishers Clearing House sweepstakes, this isn't anything you can rely on. I mean something you can do and control.

Write as many answers as come to mind. Don't just grab the first one. Usually the ones that come later are better than the one that comes immediately.

Think of the horse wearing blinders. The horse has only to move forward. Looking in every direction would just distract the horse. So put on your psychological blinders and keep those negative visions of failure from stopping you from taking action. Focus on the one next step.

Don't Stop at These Stop Signs!

Depression and anxiety can act as stop signs when you need to get going to work on problems, decisions, goals, and projects. If you're depressed, you lack the psychic energy to take action. It's called apathy. It makes it hard to get energized so you can take that first step. Or if you take that step, you feel bogged down, as though you are trudging through waist-high mud.

Even if you do something, it feels unpleasant, and the experience may prevent you from doing other things. It forms a bad memory of the problem-solving experience.

The same thing happens with anxiety (and with some people, they are both going on at once). Worrying about failure, expenses, and other dark thoughts projected into the future makes it hard to get going. The stop sign looms, and you dread what lies ahead if you move forward. If you manage to get going, you find that each step is tense and ridden with negative thoughts. Again, you're creating a bad memory of problem solving. Instead of it being fun, you think of it as a burden, a chore to be avoided. Does this sound like you?

Try This Exercise to Improve Your Mood:
Exercise 7-3: Happier Times

> Focus on a memory of yourself in happier times (or if you can't remember any happier times, project the image into the future). What were you doing? What emotions filled you? Can you see yourself today doing this? If not, can you transfer this happy image to some activity you can imagine doing?

Did this little exercise improve your mood? If not, try the next one.

Exercise 7-4: "If I Can See It, I Can Do It."

> Create an image of how you would like to be. See yourself doing the things you associate with that. In the song "I Believe I Can Fly," the writer sees himself going through an open door. The door represents something that writer wants to achieve in his life. He believes if he can see it, he can do it. So imagine yourself seeing this thing you want to do and doing it. How will you feel when you're doing it?

Did this little exercise improve your mood? If one or both exercises work, write them down on your log and return to them later. The more you practice this, the easier it gets. The more it becomes a habit, the less you have to make efforts and strain at problem solving. It will soon happen automatically.

Get Out of the Perfectionism Trap

Do you put off or avoid doing something because you believe you cannot do it well? Do you fail to finish projects because you think what you've done is not good enough? Do you go over your work repetitively seeking minute improvements?

Perfectionism can paralyze us. It can keep us from enjoying activities and finishing projects. And it annoys other people.

Life is not an endless report card, and striving to get an A+ for everything we do sucks all the joy from life.

Use Broad Brush Strokes

There is nothing wrong with striving for excellence. Perfectionism is the pathological side of the endeavor coin. A way to train yourself out of this is to create a mental image of broad brush strokes. This reminds you that you don't have to do something perfectly, just get the bulk of it done well. As a reforming perfectionist, I trained myself to say those three words. "Broad brush strokes!" now pops into my mind without effort. I might do more than just broad brush strokes, but I am not doing it with that sense of the need to do it perfectly. So there is less stress and I can accomplish things well but with less effort.

Ask yourself, is the extra effort to make it perfect worth the delay? The strain? The annoyance it causes others? Unless you are a scientist or medical doctor and lives hang in the balance, will it matter to anyone that your project was only 98% excellent?

Make your goal excellence, not perfection, if it is an important project. If it is cleaning the kitchen or dusting or mowing the lawn, go for 85%. Get comfortable with lesser degrees for the smaller projects and save your energy for the bigger ones.

If you try the techniques in this chapter and they don't seem to work to get you unstuck and back on the road, then consider seeking professional help.

Find the Right Workaround

We looked at reasons for being stuck that involved negative thinking getting in your way and causing the roadblock. But what if the problem is beyond your control, not something that a change of attitude will fix?

Do you give up and say, "I can't do this, it's impossible." No! Find a workaround. Go back to your Roadmap chart and rework the seven sections. Use the Six Thinking Hats and other techniques to come up with solutions. In the next chapter, you will find examples of people using the Personal Power Roadmap to work around problems.

Key Points in This Chapter

Negative thinking keeps you stuck. To get unstuck, you need to identify the Negative Automatic Thoughts (NATs) and remove them by arguing against them. Changing your thoughts changes your moods. Methods for removing "malware of the mind" use the 3 Essential Skills.

What You Will Learn In the Next Chapter

In the next chapter, "Applying the Personal Power Roadmap to Life's Flat Tires," I show you how to apply everything you learned so far to problems of 21st-century living. You will see how the 3 Essential Skills interact and interrelate when working with the Personal Power Roadmap.

8

Applying the Personal Power Roadmap to Life's Flat Tires

Mario and Anna wanted to sell more sandwiches, Bert wanted to buy a house, Jane wanted to find a mate, and George and Nancy wanted to end the power struggle threatening to derail a long and happy marriage.

If you were wondering how the Personal Power Roadmap could work for decision making, problem solving, goal setting and projects, you will learn how from the case histories in this chapter.

In the Introduction, I made bold statements about the Personal Power Roadmap: "You only need to learn one method, one time." I described the method as "a practical, proven multi tool for making decisions, solving problems, setting goals, and creating projects."

Now I want to show you actual cases where people, either alone or with others, worked on problems with the Personal Power Roadmap.

Case History: Solving a Business Problem

Mario and his wife Anna opened a small café in a university town. The plan was that Anna would bake pastries and make sandwiches for the café and Mario would greet customers and make drinks.

Despite their hard work, there wasn't much business except early in the morning and at lunch time, and they were just barely scraping by.

Using the Personal Power Roadmap and the START NOW questions, they phrased the problem: "Investigate and implement changes that will bring in more business and increase profits within three months."

They offered a free muffin to customers who would fill out a brief confidential questionnaire. Some questions were what they liked and disliked, whether they would recommend the café to others, and what improvements they would like to see.

They also did online research. They Googled "how to increase profits from small café" and found a lot of helpful advice. Using the results of the muffin-inspired survey and the Google search, they set up their "Next Actions" and started putting the changes into place.

They never had to use their Plan B, which was to close the café and try a catering business.

Case History: Putting a Goal Into Action

Bert longed to own a house. He had given up on buying one because he couldn't get a big enough down payment together to keep pace with inflation of the housing market in his town. He didn't qualify for a zero down payment loan. He took a course on how to buy a house without a down payment. He dutifully sent off the letter to the relative the instructor recommended where he promised to repay the down payment loan. But his "Dear Uncle John" letter produced polite regrets.

Bert tried the Personal Power Roadmap after a friend said it could help with reaching goals. He crafted this goal: "Buy my first house by the end of this year." He had no problem coming up with good reasons for wanting to reach this goal. He used the "Six Thinking Hats" technique with a friend who was a yellow hat (optimistic) and green hat (creative) type. She prepared for the session by doing some online research.

The brainstorming session produced several methods Bert had not tried, so he entered them into the Next Actions section of his Personal Power Roadmap and put each method into motion. Right before Christmas he closed on a fixer upper the owner was desperate to sell. Bert made a small down payment and took over the existing mortgage. In exchange for the low price and favorable terms, he agreed to rent part of the house to the seller for a year. It was an unconventional approach Bert never imagined, but he reached his goal on target.

Case History: Weight Loss

Susie wanted to lose the 30 pounds she had gained since graduating from college 15 years before, but she found she was frequently straying from her diet. She told me, "I just don't have any real motivation, even though I know it's important for my health and that I'll look a lot better." I asked her if she had done anything to energize her motivation. She looked at me quizzically. I explained that motivation isn't some fixed amount, but can be increased by using the two other essential skills, imagination and cognition. I asked, "Do you have a picture on your refrigerator of you 30 pounds ago?"

She said, "No, but I'm going to put one there when I get home. Maybe that will inspire me." I said, "You could also do research on the specific health benefits of being your ideal weight instead of 30 pounds over. If you do both, it will increase your motivation and that will make it easier to stick to your diet and exercise plan."

Susie set up her Personal Power Roadmap. She took a favorite outfit that used to fit her and hung it in the front of her closet, with a picture of her wearing it to her graduation party. She set a goal of going to her 20th college reunion in the graduation dress. She did the "If I can see it, I can do it" exercise from Chapter 7 each day and hummed the song "I Believe I Can Fly" when she was around food she knew would wreck her diet.

Susie did not try to crash off the 30 pounds. She knew from past efforts at dieting that crash dieting was soon followed by binge eating and additional weight gain. This time she worked on making small but regular weight loss goals, with incentives and rewards when she made each goal. She allowed herself small helpings of the "forbidden" foods she had over-indulged in before. By not denying herself these foods, but instead controlling the portions and occasions, she did not feel deprived.

Career Choices and Changes

Do you love what you do so it doesn't even seem like work?

Too often people think that picking the right career means finding the best-paid work. When dissatisfaction sets in later, they are stuck in a job they don't like or even hate and used to living on income higher than what they'd earn doing work they would rather do.

Wouldn't it be easier when you're starting out after high school or college to look for work you are passionate about and learn to live on the income it produces? But we live in a culture where having money and buying many consumer products and services is what everyone seems to do, even though it produces no sense of satisfaction or happiness if you don't like your work.

Find work you are passionate about and learn to live on the income it produces. Don't be concerned with family members or friends who are unhappy you didn't pick a high-income, status type position.

I didn't follow my own advice when I was younger. I was looking for financial security so I went into a profession I assumed would pay me decently. I put aside what I wanted to do because I didn't know if I'd be able to pay my rent and I couldn't depend on someone else's support.

It wasn't long before I realized I was stuck doing work I didn't like, so I tried some other ways to make a living. But again my worries about paying my mortgage kept me chained. Much later in life, I did things on my own terms so I could do the other things I wanted to do which brought more satisfaction but less or no income.

We get trapped by fear and financial dependence. You can use the Personal Power Roadmap to plan your escape.

To improve your career options, focus on acquiring skills for specific types of job duties. Master software that not only helps your employer but would look good on your resume if you don't get recognized and promoted at your current job. Or take a course that gives you better credentials. Focus on what you can achieve within the coming months. Don't get distracted by something that will take years to accomplish. You will never get there anyway unless you take the first step and keep taking steps after that. Recite aphorisms from Chapter 6, such as "A journey of a thousand miles begins with a single step."

Getting Free of the Money Trap

Are you making money just to have the money or as the result of doing work you love?

Why do so many people think they would be happy if they only had more money? Money can't buy love, only companionship. Money can't buy health, only good medical care. Money can't buy happiness, only creature comforts.

We can solve most of our money problems by changing our attitude about money and being happy with less.

We can also change our habits so we don't need as much money or waste as much.

Do you judge others by how much money they have or don't have? Then you probably judge yourself the same way.

So try this approach to get out of the money trap: set up a Personal Power Roadmap and label it: "I will be financially free and doing work I love by [set reasonable goal depending on how much you need to change to achieve this goal]."

Read about Joe Dominguez and Vicki Robin of the New Roadmap Foundation: www.financialintegrity.org/index.php?title=Main_Page There are nine steps and downloadable guides. If this appeals to you, I urge you to integrate it with your own Personal Power Roadmap.

Case History: Finding a Mate

Jane is 35. For the last 10 years, she has been living in San Francisco and working as an account executive for a major company. She longs to get married and have children. She tried dating coaches, online services, matchmakers, and self-help books but still has not found a mate.

Millie, Jane's best friend from college, urged her to move to a town with more men wanting to get married. Millie researched online and came up with a list.

Jane set up a Personal Power Roadmap. For "Problem" she wrote, "I want to get married and have children." She asked Millie for help. "This is too vague. This has been on your New Year's resolution list for years and nothing you've tried has worked so far," Millie said.

Jane changed it to read, "I want to find a man willing to commit and have children by the end of this year."

"Still too vague!" Millie said. "You seem to be putting this in the hands of some man you don't even know. Are *you* willing to commit? If you are, what are you going to do to find this man?"

Jane thought about it more and used the START NOW questions for phrasing the problem so it was solvable. She came up with this: "I will move to [location to be inserted after research, etc.] by the end of the year and find a decent, kind and loving man who's ready to commit to marriage and children."

After coming up with a solvable problem, Jane wrote her reasons. That part was easy. She longed to have a husband and children, to have a loving partner to share life's joys and burdens. While she loved San Francisco, it wasn't worth staying if she couldn't find what she had longed for since her teen years. She did not want to get more set in her ways and needed a change. The "cons" were the inconvenience of relocating and finding a new job and new friends.

Then Jane sat in a comfortable chair, closed her eyes, and imagined herself five years from now. Seeing herself holding a baby in her lap, her husband by her side, she was flooded with a warm fuzzy feeling. She felt loved and cherished.

Jane asked herself the questions from the Looking Backward part of the Time Travel Technique in Chapter 4.

> What do you see in your mind's eye?

> What advice would allow you in the present moment to bring about the vision you had looking forward?

> How could it help you with the Roadmap you created for this problem?

Jane wrote that looking back she saw a sad and lonely woman longing for love, not just from a mate but a child. She would advise the Jane of five years before to pursue her dream, not to give up but to put everything she had into materializing her dream. She gave that Jane a rousing pep talk and told her to increase her motivation using the techniques in Chapter 6.

Jane added this to the Roadmap under "What I imagine for the future": "I have no doubt about what I really want. I feel I can get this and I'm willing to make the efforts needed. I can see myself there. I uncovered no negative thoughts."

Millie provided a list of cities with marriage potential. Jane went online and found out as much as she could about each town. After a few hours of research, she narrowed the list to two cities. One had a branch of her company, which eliminated her concern about having to find a new job. While that would make relocating less stressful, Jane wasn't sure she could adjust to the weather in that city. The other town had a warmer climate.

Millie said, "Why don't you take vacation time and visit both places? Look at the neighborhoods you'd be living in, and the business district where you'd work. Also, check out places you'd go for fun."

Jane next researched her alumni association to see if anyone from her school lived in either town. She emailed to a former classmate, Ellen, who lived in the suburbs of the warmer city. Within days, they were chatting on the phone. Ellen was eager to show her around and hinted she might introduce her to potential mates.

Jane decided that having social contacts lined up before moving was more important than the job. With her background, she thought she could easily find a job in the warmer city.

Jane listed her next steps: 1. Plan trip to [warmer city] 2. Reserve vacation time 3. Get plane ticket.

Case History: Working on a Relationship Power Struggle

George and Nancy had been married for many years and thought of their marriage as a happy and solid one. They were both in their 40s.

They had a working dispute resolution method in place: at a designated time every week, they held a "town hall meeting" were they aired their grievances. They would address each other calmly and respectfully and announce what was upsetting and what needed to change.

Recently a new problem was threatening the relationship: Nancy was worrying about money and the future. They were barely scraping by and had no savings. George was content with his part time, low paid job working in the library. He had time to read, walk the dog in the park and chat with strangers, hang out in coffee houses and engage in long and meaningful conversations with people he met there.

Nancy was working full-time at a more stressful and better paid job but was still not earning enough to support them and save money. She wanted George to work full time so they could save.

Despite the weekly discussions, it had become a "power struggle" as Nancy put it between their different goals. George wanted to maintain the lifestyle that had worked for so long. Nancy had become "bourgeois" in his opinion.

At the weekly discussions, they were getting increasingly angry with one another. Traditionally their "town hall" ended with loving feelings and a sense of peace, but they were now "going around in circles and never getting anywhere," as Nancy put it.

They tried the Personal Power Road Map. They worked on the exercises and techniques together, starting with the Time Travel technique from Chapter 4. They separately wrote notes, then shared them.

Nancy imagined them together 10 years later. They were both working full-time at jobs they liked. They had bought a duplex, half of which they rented out while living in the other unit. The rent money paid for most of the mortgage. They were building their retirement nest egg by regularly saving 10% of their earnings.

George's vision 10 years later had them living in the same place as before, and he was still working part time at the library. But he had written and published a book about the stories people told him on his walks in the park and visits to the coffee house, and they were saving the royalties from the book.

They answered the questions from the exercise and did the Six Thinking Hats exercise from Chapter 5. They rotated through the six colored hats, each taking a turn for each color, and recorded their responses on the Six Thinking Hats mind map. They liked the exercise so much they do it for their weekly "town halls." Wearing the red hat, Nancy expressed frustration and resentment at George's lack of ambition, and George expressed resentment at Nancy's nagging. Nancy also expressed fear for the future.

Wearing the black hat, Nancy wrote, "There's no way to save money unless George works harder. We face dire poverty in old age." She added: "George's vision of making money from a book is a fantasy. It will just take up a lot of time to write and probably won't make any money."

For the yellow hat, George wrote: "We will be able to get by and enjoy our lives when we are too old to work." "My book is like *Chicken Soup for the Soul* and should make a lot of money."

They separately wrote answers to the START NOW questions. They used the mind map format for their Roadmap and recorded their answers there. After research and analysis of options, they listed steps they could each take to improve their ability to save for the future. This included reading the guides they found on the New Roadmap Foundation website (www.financialintegrity.org/index.php?title=Downloadable_Guides).

Using the chart, exercises, and techniques in this book, this couple could limit the disharmony over money and take practical steps to allay Nancy's fears for a poverty ridden future. Nancy felt they had achieved a "balance of power" and diminished the "power struggle" over the financial results of George's lifestyle choices. She now had a plan they could both work on, and George was relieved that she was no longer nagging him about his lack of ambition.

Case History: Decluttering the Guest Room

When I moved to my current house, I was determined not to have a "junk room." I had a big garage so why would I need a junk room anyway? After a few years, I found that stuff was accumulating in various rooms, so I temporarily put things in the guest room.

I did a great job decluttering the other rooms (a New Year's resolution), but I ended up with a junk room and no guest room. The "declutter the garage" project had fallen by the wayside, so there was no room to move the clutter from the guest room to the garage. Every time I opened the guest room door, I was dismayed by the huge task of sorting out a mountain of cartons and plastic garbage bags.

I knew I would never do it if I tried to do it all in one day. There was no one day I could devote to such an unpleasant chore. I'd have to do it in chunks.

I set up a Personal Power Roadmap using the Evernote template. The Problem: "Clean out the guest room by April 1 so I can have company visit." The reasons:

- A clean and neat house is important to my self-esteem
- It means I can have company over on the fly
- I won't leave an inordinate mess for my executor

Under "What I imagine for the future" I inserted a picture of the room before it became the junk room.

I didn't need to fill in "Research and Analysis" because I knew how to do this from techniques I learned years before (like having three piles, "keep," "toss," "give away"). But I Googled "declutter house" and got good ideas to apply to other rooms and the garage.

There was no Plan B. I could not let a 11' by 11' room defeat me.

Next I filled in "To Do" with due dates under "Next Actions." I went into the room for 15 minutes and just looked, getting an idea in my mind of where to begin. I realized if I could consolidate many cartons they would take up less space and be less intimidating. I brought in some empty cartons and trash bags to make it easier to sort out what was there.

In 15 minutes, I made an appreciable difference and had started the sorting process. I determined to spend 15 minutes the next day.

The first progress log entry read: "I tackled the guest room this evening. I could move out a bunch of things and came up with a plan for moving the bookshelf to the garage. I just need to move the card table in the garage, fold it up and put it against the wall, and the bookshelf will then fit in there."

The project went so well, I was soon motivated to stay in the room for over 15 minutes. As the pile shrunk, I recorded my progress with smartphone photos and linked them to my log. By the end of a week, I had finished this project and emailed to the friend I wanted to come visit. The subject line said "Buya! The guestroom is ready. "I included a picture of the room, now cleared of everything that had accumulated for all those months.

Case History: Ending a Bad Habit and Establishing Good Ones

Sometimes we struggle with stopping a bad habit because we are afraid it could cause a new problem. Dorothy knew she should stop smoking, but she feared she'd gain weight. She was more worried about being fat than being fit. Her friend Greg persuaded her to try again, this time using the Personal Power Roadmap. He offered to do it with her, to be her "accountability buddy" although he did not smoke.

Using the Roadmap chart and the Four Thinking Hats to End Procrastination from Chapter 7, Dorothy explored with Greg why she continued to smoke despite the health warnings and feeling like a social pariah as friends flung open windows when she lit up. It was not just the fear of weight gain stopping Dorothy. She feared failure. She also felt she was too stressed out to give up her cigarettes, which she claimed had a calming effect.

Greg then presented his research to her. He had Googled "do cigarettes calm your nerves?" and learned there was a temporary calming effect because smoking relieves withdrawal symptoms. He also showed her the results from Googling "quit smoking without gaining weight."

After demolishing her reasons for not quitting, Greg volunteered to go on daily "power walks" with Dorothy. Dorothy listed on the first section of her Roadmap, "Quit smoking by the end of January without gaining weight by exercising and eating a filling, low-calorie diet." She listed under "Next Actions": take daily walks and munch on raw veggies and fruits when I'm hungry." In the Progress Log, she made daily notes about what she had eaten and how much she had exercised.

In a month, Dorothy was free of the bad habit and had instituted two good ones – daily exercise and a healthier diet. She did not gain weight. She also felt calmer than when she smoked.

Some Takeaways

Decide as soon as a problem arises or you think of changing your life, what type of plan you need. Some problems have many moving parts and are projects with subprojects. Some problems are vague, one big ball of wax. Some, like decluttering a room, are small with few moving parts.

Some problems benefit from making a list, and others from creating an image. Some combine both. Anything that takes place over time – more than a few hours or a day – and you have resistance to doing will benefit from using the Personal Power Roadmap. By writing something, doing exercises and applying techniques and research, you tell yourself, "This is important to me."

Be proactive and foresee coming changes. Read news about your industry. If you work in an industry that will change soon, study ways to improve your position. You will need to adjust to changing times to keep your job. Be the same about relationships: notice when changes require you to go into action. Many relationships end because people drift away, not noticing that the other seems to have lost interest, or because the couple is avoiding rather than addressing problems. If you keep putting off goals, is it because they are not important to you, or just that your negative thoughts are controlling your life?

Often our problems or goals require us to change our habits. If we focus on achieving something by a certain date, we can lose sight of the daily "next actions" we need to do to reach the goal. Make sure you log your practice at least weekly on the seventh section of your Roadmap, the Progress Log.

Key Points in This Chapter

The Personal Power Roadmap is flexible and works for decision making, problem solving, goal setting and creating projects. It can be used by one or more people. When a problem arises, don't delay in planning a response. By writing it down, doing exercises and applying techniques and research, you tell yourself, "This is important to me." Be proactive and foresee coming changes.

What You Will Learn In the Next Chapter

In the next chapter, "The Challenge of Change," I tell you about two remarkable mentors who taught me much of what I know about decision making, problem solving, and goal setting. They believed through hard work and determination, you could reinvent your life.

9

The Challenge of Change

Some people significantly change their lives, move around the world, reinvent themselves, and influence many others. They seem, in retrospect, to have a clear vision of what they want to accomplish and then it just happens, as if by magic.

It Doesn't Happen by Magic

If you know such people intimately and know of their struggles, or you're able to read a biography later, you learn they had their dark moments, where they were engulfed in mental fog, where they couldn't see where they wanted to go or how to do it. But they persisted, they overcame the dark thoughts, they followed a vision and became people who others later wrote about.

Maybe some wrote down the process they were following, what steps they wanted to take and what they did. Or perhaps their vision took up so much of their conscious mind they did not have to record their process.

For most of us, it helps to have a system we can follow, something that reminds us of what we need to do, what we need to think about. It is for those people I created the Personal Power Roadmap. I am one person who needs such a system and uses it.

There were two remarkable men from whom I learned much of what I know about problem solving, decision making, and goal setting. One I knew only in a professional capacity. I learned more about his personal life later from his obituary and from a book his daughter wrote. But I know enough about him from my contact with him to know that solving life's problems takes effort, repeated often, and is difficult, but not impossible.

Both my problem-solving mentors were members of the generations called to serve in world wars. They both believed you could reinvent your life. They both moved from their birthplaces, took on big challenges, went through hard and harrowing times, and influenced many by their teachings.

They modeled the START NOW method, approaching decisions, problems, and goals with the components in mind. They did not call it that, nor did I back then. Looking back now, I see the traits that brought them success. They both focused on what really was and did not let negative thoughts become their reality. They had a clear vision of what they wanted to achieve. That vision motivated them to work hard and persist.

"Problems Are an Opportunity to Have Fun"

When I first heard this from Harland Hand, I didn't myself believe this. In my mind, "problems" are something bad, not "fun." In time, I understood what he meant. He had trained his mind to see problems as challenges, as opportunities for creativity. That's what made them "fun."

It wasn't always fun, and not always creative, but by adopting that attitude, Hand could move forward rapidly when confronted with problems. There were decisions he never made, there were goals he never reached, but he accomplished most of what he wanted to in his lifetime and worked on being positive, forward-looking and energetic.

In Chapter 2 I talked about Hand's experience in combat in World War II, and how a lesson he learned from Aunt Mary – how to focus on what had to be done right at that moment – helped him survive.

In his poem "War Lessons," he described his way of confronting the terror of war or later dark moments:

> I must deal with things
>
> as they are and as I can.
>
> For when I see that whatever is,
>
> is exactly what it is,
>
> I can fight away the dungeons
>
> of trivia and paralyzing fear.

(Reprinted by permission of Emma Lou Schley, executor of Mr. Hand's estate.)

Hand had a remarkable ability to focus his mind. I witnessed this during a terrifying road trip in Greece. I thought death was imminent and wished for a magic carpet to miraculously transport us to safety. Harland gripped the wheel, gritted his teeth and drove.

He often spoke of his Aunt Mary and how she got things done. He admired her determined attitude. He encouraged me to move forward with projects and not be deterred by negative thoughts. When I expressed worry about opening my own law practice and surviving economically, he said, "Someday you will look back on this as the best decision you ever made." Years later, when I was doing well financially, he said, "I always knew you would make as much money as you needed."

Hand grew up during the depression, survived one of history's greatest battles, was one of the troops that liberated concentration camps, and then returned to peacetime America to get on with his life. He wanted to make gardens, but it took time to get the money and the plot of land so his vision could become concrete. He used concrete to create a remarkable garden in El Cerrito, California, where I lived for seven and half years. Two years after his death, I moved there to renovate the garden, which, as another friend said, "had lost its sparkle."

While toiling on the steep hillside, rescuing the concrete structures from encroaching weeds, I understood more deeply just how stunning Harland Hand's accomplishment was. He broke the conventions of landscape architecture and horticulture, let no contrary opinions affect his optimism and overcame moments of negativity by focusing on his vision. It took the better part of 20 years to get to the bottom of the property and complete the concrete work, after which he was up at the top again, repairing the unsuccessful parts where the concrete had crumbled.

In an unpublished manuscript (*The Composed Garden: A Personal View of the Western Garden as Fine-Art*) Hand wrote, "Mistakes and experiments can seem costly, but, so far, I have found the knowledge gained so satisfying and the final results so exciting that it has been worth the cost many times over."

What Hand said about garden construction is equally valid for other areas of endeavor. Problem solving and change, the hoped-for outcome of the process, can be a bumpy road. The more difficult the journey, the greater the satisfaction when you reach your destination.

Like Harland's garden building, when you get to the end, you go back again and start on a new project. You get better each time, pack lighter and move faster. Do it with the mindset of the baby learning to walk, or the parent holding out arms to catch the child who embodies hope for the future. Do it with determination and joy, always remembering, nothing changes unless you make changes.

Change is "Difficult But Not Impossible"

When I was in my early 20s, beset by doubts and procrastination, I was struggling to figure out what I wanted, what I should do, how to get on with my life. Although to others I appeared successful and accomplished, I was inwardly filled with negative thoughts and a sense of failure. I sought a therapist.

I was a graduate student with limited funds, so I was accepted as a clinic patient. Dr. Leslie John Adkins was assigned to be my therapist, and for three years I dutifully reported for sessions where I argued with him, resisted his suggestions, but ultimately saw the wisdom of his advice. When I left for London with my then husband, I told Dr. Adkins I considered him a miracle worker. He said, with characteristic modesty, "You must always remain vigilant. You have to actively fight negative thoughts." We stayed in touch once or twice a year from 1969 to 1991, when he died.

Often over the three years I was Dr. Adkin's patient he said in response to my negative statements, "It's difficult but not impossible." I would anticipate his saying this and sometimes beat him to it: "I know, it's difficult but not impossible" and we would both laugh.

It was not until many years later, when I studied for a master's in psychology, that I appreciated how ahead of his times Dr. Adkins was. He embraced the then-new theory of cognitive therapy, which I told you about in Chapter 7. He didn't find it helpful to discuss Freudian theories, which I frequently brought up. He would laugh and say, "I think of that as cocktail party chit chat." I couldn't envision this man at a cocktail party, chatting about Freud, so I took it to mean he put little stock in Freudian theory. He wanted me to focus on what I could do to change my mood, and to root out the negative automatic thoughts (NATs) that populated my inner world.

In the years after I left his presence, I would have imaginary conversations with him. When something soured in my life, I would ask myself, "What would Dr. Adkins say?" The frequent response was "It may be difficult, but it's not impossible."

Another favorite admonition was, "You are trying to make a silk purse out of a sow's ear." Dr. Adkins was from England and I was a city girl, but I soon realized he was referring to my boyfriends as "sow's ears" and trying to get me to see there was no way a stable relationship could come out of my poor choices.

Dr. Adkins encouraged me to try things I was sure would fail, like standing up to my parents. He would say, "How do you know it won't work when you haven't tried it?" I heard myself saying the same things years later to my clients.

When I was his patient, I knew little of his personal history, although he shared a few details with me. Years later, thanks to the Internet, I learned what a remarkable past he had. He was a minister, then a missionary in the Middle East, then a pastor, and in his 50s left the ministry and became a psychologist. He died at 92, having just completed the book he told me about in his last letter when he was 91.

The Importance of Mentors

A mentor is a wise advisor, someone we admire and trust. We want to be like them in certain ways. We want to pass on to others the lessons we learned from them.

Both of my mentors focused on what works, getting to it, seeing the possible where others saw the impossible. My mentors and I believed in the American dream. We could become what we imagined if we would do the hard work to turn the dream into actuality. Both men modeled that we can all reinvent ourselves and create masterpieces if we don't limit ourselves with "shoulds" and other negative beliefs.

Key Points in This Chapter

There were two remarkable men from whom I learned much of what I know about problem solving, decision making, and goal setting. My mentors and I believed in the American dream. We could reinvent ourselves or become what we imagined if we would do the hard work to turn the dream into actuality.

Conclusion

I hope your experience with the Personal Power Roadmap helps you solve problems, make decisions, set goals, and create projects leading to meaningful change and a better life. The results you achieve are in direct proportion to the effort you expend. It is not enough to read the book. You need to take action. Only then do you achieve the change you desire.

Remember this: the 3 Essential Skills plus the Personal Power Roadmap equal success. There is no magic carpet or magic wand, no easy way to achieve great things in life. But there are easier ways to get there. It's always easier with a tried and true system.

I hope this book has encouraged you to think of problem solving, decision making, and goal setting as a creative and imaginative process. Even if you don't find it fun at the time you're in the midst of a problem, I hope you can look back later with a sense of accomplishment and high self-esteem for having succeeded.

I encourage you to make the Personal Power Roadmap a regular part of your life and to work with the charts, the START NOW questions, and the exercises and techniques in this book.

If you would like to tell me about your experiences and your suggestions for future editions of this book, please email me at marjory@personalpowerroadmap.com. For information about my services, other publications, and weekly blog posts, visit my website: PersonalPowerRoadmap.com.

If you enjoyed this book, please leave a review on Amazon so you can help others learn how they can benefit from this book and help me learn how I can better serve my readers. One of the joys of teaching problem solving is learning how others were helped and ways I can improve. Thanks in advance to the kind readers who spread the word.

About The Author

Marjory Harris finds problem solving fascinating, as long as it does not involve math. She got her first self-help book, Dale Carnegie's *How to Win Friends and Influence People*, at age 10, after being bullied at summer camp. After graduating from Barnard College and getting a master's degree in Italian Literature from Columbia University, she was in publishing in New York City and also did a stint as a social worker. While working on a doctorate in Italian Literature, she switched to law. Since 1974, she has been practicing law in California, while also writing articles and editing medical-legal magazines. In the early 1990's, after obtaining a master's in psychology and studying hypnotherapy, Marjory developed Multidimensional Problem Solving[sm], to teach clients the techniques in this book. A longtime resident of San Francisco, she moved from the fog to sunny Loma Linda, CA, where she practices law, writes books, and gardens.

Index of Key Points, Exercises, Techniques & Case Histories

Key Points

Chapter 1: The Personal Power Roadmap is a flexible multi tool that works on many types of problems, decisions, goals or projects. It is a practical, proactive method that relies on the power of potentiation, the synergistic interaction between two or more of the 3 Essential Skills. We are born with these Essential Skills – imagination, cognition, and motivation. You have them but need to hone them.

By practicing the 3 Essential Skills with the techniques and exercises in this book, you can avoid the School of Hard Knocks and go straight to creating a personal Roadmap that will have you traveling with a new, productive itinerary.

Chapter 2: You can learn the methods and habits of successful problem solvers. Start with a solvable problem. Focus on the present. The Personal Power Roadmap is a valuable, go-to multi tool, fundamental to your success. Using the 3 Essential Skills, follow the seven steps to working with the Personal Power Roadmap, beginning with the START NOW questions.

Chapter 3: The Roadmap is an essential tool for creating change in your life. The Roadmap is not just for "problems": Use START NOW with the Roadmap to plan and track effective decision making, problem solving, goal setting, and project creation.

Chapter 4: Imagination is the ability to create a mental image. This skill allows you to break free from linear thinking and encourages related or unrelated ideas to emerge from the unconscious mind. We explored four techniques with variations: time travel, bypassing the conscious censor, using fantasies to create reality, and mind mapping. You imagined yourself in a future time and place so you could use that image to design your Roadmap.

Chapter 5: Cognition is the ability to use conscious processes to reason, analyze, research, and document your efforts. "Lateral thinking" is creating new perceptions and new concepts instead of following the linear thinking in use since antiquity. You can use de Bono's Six Thinking Hats technique to separate the thought processes. By compartmentalizing the different thought processes, you may come up with creative solutions. You can acquire knowledge readily using Internet search engines and store and categorize what you learned in Evernote or in a file box with hanging folders.

Chapter 6: We were all born with the essential skill of motivation. We can increase this by using imagination and cognition. You need a reason that creates a desire, one you fully support, one consistent with your core values and priorities, not someone else's. Rewards, treats or incentives are visions of the future. They function as magnets, pulling you toward your goal. You can gain momentum with pep talks, motivational quotes and music. An anchor image or word uses imagination and cognition to keep you motivated to achieve success.

Chapter 7: Negative thinking keeps you stuck. To get unstuck, you need to identify the Negative Automatic Thoughts (NATs) and remove them by arguing against them. Changing your thoughts changes your moods. Methods for removing "malware of the mind" use the 3 Essential Skills.

Chapter 8: The Personal Power Roadmap is flexible and works for decision making, problem solving, goal setting and creating projects. It can be used by one or more people. When a problem arises, don't delay in planning a response. By writing it down, doing exercises and applying techniques and research, you tell yourself, "This is important to me." Be proactive and foresee coming changes.

Chapter 9: There were two remarkable men from whom I learned much of what I know about problem solving, decision making, and goal setting. My mentors and I believed in the American dream. We could reinvent ourselves or become what we imagined if we would do the hard work to turn the dream into actuality.

Exercises

Learning to Walk: Ch. 1

Planning a Vacation: Ch. 1

Food Aisle Temptation: Ch. 1

Breaking Eggs: Ch. 1

Happiness: Ch. 1

On the Train: Ch. 1

Unexpected Loss of Job: Ch. 2

Changing Your Life: Ch. 4

Techniques

Cognition: Ch. 5

5. Six Thinking Hats

6. How to Make a Roadmap in a Box

7. How to use Evernote

8. How to Analyze Your Research and Incorporate it Into Your Personal Power Roadmap

Motivation: Ch. 6

9. Create an Anchor Image or Word

10. Six Thinking Hats

11. Select a Reward, Treat, or Incentive to Increase Motivation

12. Affirmations, Aphorisms, Words of Hope, Mantras, or Motivational Quotes

13. Create a Winning Pep Talk

14. Inspiring Music (YouTube "Motivational Music")

Getting Unstuck: Ch. 7

15. Mind Map Using 4 Thinking Hats

16. End Procrastination with the Four Thinking Hats Technique

17. One Step

Case Histories

The Personal Power Roadmap in 4 formats

The following screenshots show the 4 formats, with the Word template in two layouts, landscape and portrait. You can download the documents at www.personalpowerroadmap.com/templates

Personal Power Roadmap

Problem:[1] START NOW			
Reasons[2]	Pros		Cons
	Potential Roadblocks & Opportunity Cost		Core Values & Priorities
What I imagine for the future			
Research & Analysis[3]	Research		Analysis
Plan B[4]			

Next Actions[5]	To Do	Due Date
	☐	
	☐	
	☐	
	☐	
	☐	
	☐	
	☐	
	☐	
	☐	

Progress Log	Date	What I did to advance solution/change	Notes

1 Is the problem/decision/goal/project defined so it is solvable and doable? Is it specific? Does it contain an action? Is it realistic? Does it have a date? Use START NOW:

- Specific
- Timeframe
- Actionable & Appreciable
- Realistic
- Thrilling
- Now
- Open
- Workable

2. What reasons motivate you to act? What stops you from taking action? What obstacles impede your journey?

3. Is there more you need to know? Update this as needed.

4. Create a separate Personal Power Roadmap if necessary

5. Break the actions down so they are bite-sized and doable. Calendar these actions. Set realistic deadlines.

Notes on using Word template: Insert additional lines by right clicking on row, Insert, Insert Row Above (or below).

Personal·Power·Roadmap¶

Problem¶		
START·NOW¶		
Reasons¶	Pros¶	Cons¶
¶	¶	¶
¶	¶	¶
¶	¶	¶
¶	¶	¶
¶	¶	¶
¶	¶	¶
¶	Potential·Roadblocks·&·Opportunity·Cost¶	Core·Values·&·Priorities¶
¶	¶	¶
¶	¶	¶
¶	¶	¶
What·I·imagine·for·the·future¶	¶	
Research·&·Analysis¶	Research¶	Analysis¶
¶	¶	¶
¶	¶	¶
¶	¶	¶
¶	¶	¶
¶	¶	¶

¶	¶	¶
Plan·B¶	¶	¶
Next·Actions¶	To·Do¶	Due·Date¶
¶	☐¶	¶
¶	☐¶	¶
¶	☐¶	¶
¶	☐¶	¶
¶	☐¶	¶
¶	☐¶	¶
¶	☐¶	¶
¶	☐¶	¶

Progress·Log¶	Date¶	What·I·did·to·advance·solution/change¶	Notes¶
¶	¶	¶	¶
¶	¶	¶	¶
¶	¶	¶	¶
¶	¶	¶	¶
¶	¶	¶	¶
¶	¶	¶	¶
¶	¶	¶	¶
¶	¶	¶	¶

¶
1·Is·the·problem/decision/goal/project·defined·so·it·is·solvable·and·doable?·Is·it·specific?·Does·it·contain·an·action?·Is·it·realistic?¶ Does·it·have·a·date?·Use·START·NOW:¶
¶
• → Specific¶
• → Timeframe¶
• → Actionable·&·Appreciable¶
• → Realistic¶

• → Thrilling¶
• → Now¶
• → Open¶
• → Workable¶
¶
2·What·reasons·motivate·you·to·act?·What·stops·you·from·taking·action?·What·obstacles·impede·your·journey?¶
3·Is·there·more·you·need·to·know?·Update·this·as·needed.¶
4·Create·a·separate·Personal·Power·Roadmap·if·necessary¶
5·Break·the·actions·down·so·they·are·bite-sized·and·doable.·Calendar·these·actions.·Set·realistic·deadlines.¶
¶
Notes·on·using·Word·template·Insert·additional·lines·by·right·clicking·on·row,·Insert,·Insert·Row·Above·(or·below).¶

Personal Power Roadmap

Problem¹ START NOW			
Reasons²	**Pros**		**Cons**
	Potential Roadblocks & Opportunity Cost		**Core Values & Priorities**
What I imagine for the future			
Research & Analysis³	**Research**		**Analysis**
Plan B⁴			
Next Actions⁵	**To Do**		**Due Date**
	☐		
	☐		
	☐		
	☐		
	☐		
	☐		
Progress Log	**Date**	**What I did to advance solution/change**	**Notes**

1 Is the problem/decision/goal/project defined so it is solvable and doable? Is it specific? Does it contain an action? Is it realistic? Does it have a date? Use START NOW:

- Specific
- Timeframe
- Actionable & Appreciable
- Realistic
- Thrilling
- Now
- Open
- Workable

2. What reasons motivate you to act? What stops you from taking action? What obstacles impede your journey?
3. Is there more you need to know? Update this as needed.
4. Create a separate Personal Power Roadmap if necessary
5. Break the actions down so they are bite-sized and doable. Calendar those actions. Set realistic deadlines.

Notes on using Word template: Insert additional lines by right clicking on row, Insert, Insert Row Above (or below).

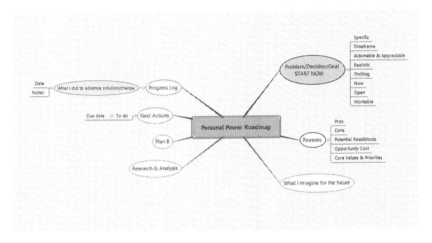

The Personal Power Roadmap as a Mind Map

On the next page there's a screenshot of the Personal Power Roadmap in Evernote. The Evernote template is also available in sections.

The Personal Power Roadmap Template - Evernote

File   Edit   View   Note   Format   Tools   Help

Reminder   Present   Print   Info   Share   Email   Delete

11 A Little Book for Big Problems   Click to add tag...

Created: 2/10/2016 2:24 PM   Updated: 2/10/2016 2:28 PM

What I imagine for the future			
Research & Analysis[3]	Research	Analysis	
Plan B[4]			

Next Actions[5]	To Do		Due Date
☐			
☐			
☐			
☐			
☐			
☐			
☐			
☐			
☐			

Progress Log	Date	What I did to advance solution/change	Notes

1 Is the problem/decision/goal/project defined so it is solvable and doable? Is it specific? Does it contain an action? Is it realistic? Does it have a date? Use START NOW:

- **Specific**
- **Timeframe**
- **Actionable & Appreciable**
- **Realistic**
- **Thrilling**
- **Now**
- **Open**
- **Workable**

2. What reasons motivate you to act? What stops you from taking action? What obstacles impede your journey?
3. Is there more you need to know? Update this as needed.
4. Create a separate Personal Power Roadmap if necessary
5. Break the actions down so they are bite-sized and doable. Calendar these actions. Set realistic deadlines.

Author's Note

Thank you for investing in yourself and in this book. You can stay in touch with me by making sure you receive The Personal Power Roadmap newsletter. Just go to www.personalpowerroadmap.com and provide your email address.

For the Roadmap chart in 4 formats:
www.personalpowerroadmap.com/templates

To download the mind maps and see screenshots of the ones from this book: www.personalpowerroadmap.com/mind-maps

Instructions on how to use The Personal Power Roadmap with Evernote: www.personalpowerroadmap.com/evernote-ppr

For the "START NOW" questions in a 2-page chart:
www.personalpowerroadmap.com/start-now

If you enjoyed this book and feel it will help others, please share the word. What goes around comes around: I wrote this book to help others and share what I learned from others.

If you're interested in personal coaching using the Personal Power Roadmap system, please contact me at: marjory@personalpowerroadmap.com.

I occasionally offer discounted sessions for those in need or who have problems in areas I am writing about in upcoming versions of the book. I will hold whatever you tell me in strict confidence.

Marjory Harris
Loma Linda, CA
April 2016

Made in the USA
Middletown, DE
12 May 2017